Ch

ISLANDS

HarperCollins*Publishers*

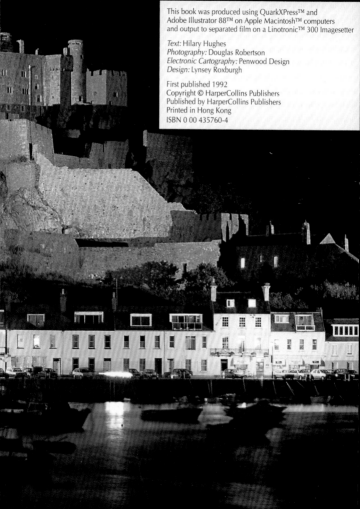

This book was produced using QuarkXPress™ and
Adobe Illustrator 88™ on Apple Macintosh™ computers
and output to separated film on a Linotronic™ 300 Imagesetter

Text: Hilary Hughes
Photography: Douglas Robertson
Electronic Cartography: Penwood Design
Design: Lynsey Roxburgh

First published 1992
Copyright © HarperCollins Publishers
Published by HarperCollins Publishers
Printed in Hong Kong
ISBN 0 00 435760-4

HOW TO USE THIS BOOK

Your Collins Traveller Guide will help you find your way around your holiday destination quickly and easily. It is split into two sections which are colour-coded:

The blue section provides you with an alphabetical sequence of headings by island, from **ALDERNEY-WHAT TO SEE** to **SARK-WHAT TO SEE** via **GUERNSEY-SHOPPING**, **HERM-WHAT TO SEE**, **JERSEY-RESTAURANTS**, etc. Each entry within a topic includes information on how to get there, how much it will cost you, when it will be open and what to expect. Furthermore, every page has its own map showing the position of each item and the nearest landmark. This allows you to orientate yourself quickly and easily in your new surroundings. To find what you want to do – having dinner, visiting a museum, going for a walk or sightseeing – simply flick through the blue headings and take your pick!

The red section is an alphabetical list of information. It provides essential facts about places and cultural items – 'What is *vraic*?', 'When is the Battle of Flowers?', 'Where are The Casquets?' – and expands on subjects touched on in the first half of the book. This section also contains practical travel information. It ranges through how to find accommodation, tips on driving, the variety of eating places and food available, information on money, which newspapers are available and where to find water-sports facilities. It is lively and informative and easy to use. Each band shows the first three letters of the first entry on the page. Simply flick through the bands till you find the entry you need!

All the main entries are also cross-referenced to help you find them. Names in small capitals – **JERSEY-MUSEUMS** – tell you that there is more information about the item you are looking for under the topic on museums on Jersey in the first part of the book. So when you read 'see **JERSEY-MUSEUMS**' you turn to the blue heading for **JERSEY-MUSEUMS**. The instruction 'see **A-Z**' after a word, lets you know that the word has its own entry in the second part of the book. Similarly words in bold type – **Cattle** – also let you know that there is an entry in the A-Z for the indicated name. In both cases you just look under the appropriate heading in the red section.

Packed full of information and easy to use – you'll always know where you are with your Collins Traveller Guide.

The following text labels appear on the map:

LA SEIGNEURIE & GARDENS

rue de Rade

rue du Sermo

La Vaurocque

Mill Lane

OLD MILL

Dixcart Lane

Havre Gosselin

PILCHER MONUMENT

LA GRANDE GRÈVE

LA COUPÉE

DI

Pot Bay

INTRODUCTION

The Channel Islands have long been a favourite destination for mainlanders looking for a holiday that offers the sense of adventure usually associated with going abroad without the hassle of a foreign language, difficult money and strange food. These islands offer the added bonus of being well to the south of even the most favoured spots on England's Channel coast which often means much more sunshine and warmth. Conversely, they are also much visited by the French who can see them from their own country and yet know that they exude a certain Britishness which draws them over.

But none of these islands is actually a part of the United Kingdom, although they are closely allied to it. Historically this is because they were part of William of Normandy's estates when he invaded England in 1066. In 1204 the Norman mainland territories were lost to France but the islands have remained loyal to the Crown ever since.

The sense of history throughout the islands is accentuated by their systems of government which are distinct and unique. The Bailiwicks of Jersey and Guernsey manage the affairs of the islands quite independently of Parliament but are answerable to the Queen alone by way of the Lieutenant-Governor who is her official representative. If you get the chance to attend a session of any of the islands' governmental or legislative assemblies it will give you a glimpse of an interesting alternative to the familiar British procedures.

Jersey is the largest of the Channel Islands and attracts most visitors. It is well known for its tax exiles, wealthy people who make the most of the low rates of income tax set by the States of Jersey, but there is a large farming community here amongst the 85,000 strong population as well as migrant workers, fishermen and everyday Jersey folk who work in the thriving business world of St. Helier and in the burgeoning tourist trade. At only 45 square miles it is a small island to support such a large population, but there is a surprising amount of open space, particularly in the north and around the coasts. St. Helier is also a magnet for inveterate shoppers – there is no VAT to pay and many interesting continental goods are available here which don't appear in the average UK

St. Peter Port, Guernsey

High Street. This is also the island for you if you like sophisticated nightlife, high-class hotels and internationally famous cuisine.

The beauty of the Channel Islands is that they offer every shade of atmosphere. If Jersey offers high-flown pleasures, then Guernsey is not far behind but it is quieter and perhaps less flamboyant. The Bailiwick of Guernsey includes all the remaining islands – Alderney, Sark, Herm and Jethou as well as Guernsey itself and all the rocks which show their heads above water in between. Alderney offers even fewer man-made treats but it is here that the delights of island life start to make themselves felt. Sark and Herm, too, are so small that you are immediately aware of the difficulties involved in getting there, the importance of the tiniest changes in the weather and the effect this has on communications, on what will grow in the fields and gardens, on the livelihood and demeanour of the islanders, on the availability of fresh food and

practically every other aspect of life in a remote place. The smaller the island the more you will be thrown on your own resources. If you are happy to bird-watch, walk, sunbathe and swim, take boat trips and be well looked after in locally run hotels then Alderney and Sark will give you plenty of scope.

Since Victorian times the Channel Islands have been well known for their dairy produce, glasshouse tomatoes, early flowers and new potatoes. Fishermen on all the islands bring in a vast array of seafood and when these elements are combined with a residual French flair for cooking and an influx of continental chefs, it is not surprising that food in the Channel Islands is generally of an extremely high standard.

If you can't resist the fact that France is so close there are plenty of opportunities for day trips or longer excursions and it is also possible to make a round trip from UK-France-Channel Islands-UK, but it would be essential to book well ahead, particularly in the height of the summer season and especially if you want to take a vehicle with you. One of the major charms of Sark is the complete ban on cars and this brings it home to visitors that walking, cycling, taking local transport, riding horses and going by boat are really a much better bet. You will find yourself nearer to the islanders, to the islands themselves and their individuality, to the wildlife and to the sea which plays such an important part in the island life.

Rocquaine Bay, Guernsey

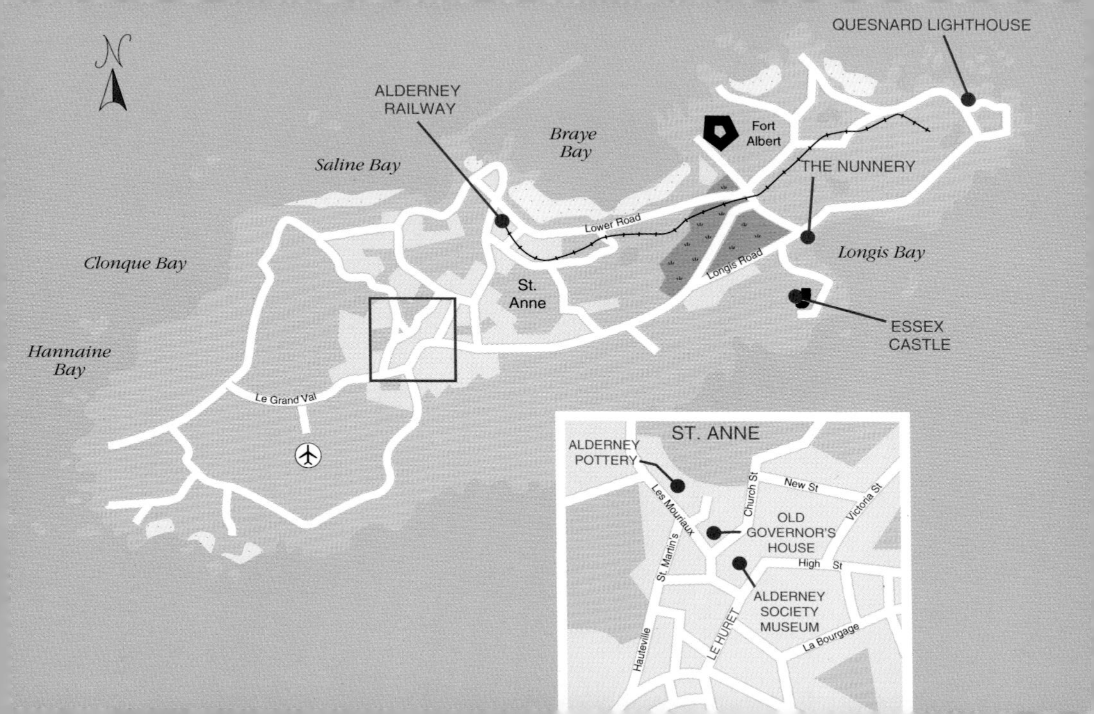

QUESNARD LIGHTHOUSE

THE NUNNERY

Longis Bay

ESSEX CASTLE

Fort Albert

Braye Bay

Lower Road

Longis Road

ALDERNEY RAILWAY

St. Anne

Saline Bay

Le Grand Val

Clonque Bay

Hannaine Bay

ST. ANNE

Victoria St

New St

Church St

High St

La Boutargue

OLD GOVERNOR'S HOUSE

ALDERNEY SOCIETY MUSEUM

ALDERNEY POTTERY

Les Mouriaux

St. Martin's St

LE HURET

Hauteville

ALDERNEY SOCIETY MUSEUM Old School, Lower High St, St. Anne, tel: 3222. ❏ 1000-1200 Mon.-Sat. ❏ £1, child under 18 free. *Displays feature the island's geology and natural history (see **A-Z**), and there are cultural items dating back to prehistoric times (see **Prehistory**).*

ALDERNEY POTTERY Les Mouriaux, St. Anne, tel: 2246. ❏ 0900-1700 Mon.-Sat., 1400-1700 Sun. in summer. ❏ Free. *Daily demonstrations; paintings and knitwear for sale as well as pots.*

OLD GOVERNOR'S HOUSE Connaught Sq., St. Anne. ❏ 1000-1630 Mon.-Fri. ❏ Donation. *This splendid building is now the island hall and library.*

LE HURET Between Marais Sq. and High St, St. Anne. *This was the open-air site of the first courts on the island, and proclamations are still made here.*

ALDERNEY RAILWAY Braye Terminus. ❏ Sat., Sun. and bank hol., summer only. ❏ £1.50, child 75p. *Steam and diesel locomotives, maintained by the Alderney Railway Society, run half-hourly through the heart of the island. See **Railways**.*

THE NUNNERY Longis Bay. ❏ Private property; not open to the public. *Never actually a religious building at all, the Nunnery was probably originally a 4thC Roman fort built to protect a port at Longis.*

ESSEX CASTLE Longis. ❏ Private property; not open to the public. *Built by Henry VIII in 1546 as part of his defences against the French on the site of a prehistoric grave complete with bones and bronze tools.*

QUESNARD LIGHTHOUSE Quesnard Point. ❏ Occasional guided tours; check with the tourist office. *Over 100 ft above sea level and visible up to 28 nautical miles away, the light guides ships through the treacherous waters of Alderney Race.*

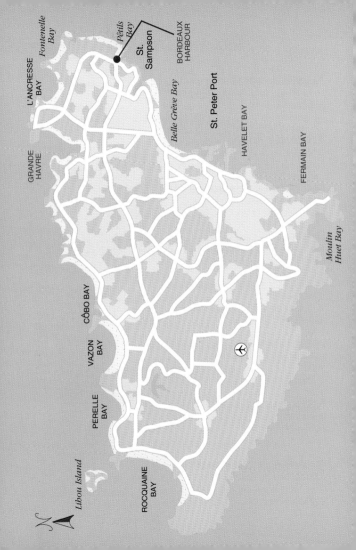

HAVELET BAY St. Peter Port.
Very convenient for town and with plenty of water-sports facilities.

FERMAIN BAY St. Martin.
Bus B. Ferry from St. Peter Port.
Secluded, southeast-facing beach with plenty of sand at low tide.

ROCQUAINE BAY St. Pierre du Bois.
Bus C, D, E, K.
Backed by a huge sea wall, this is the main surfing beach on Guernsey.

PERELLE BAY St. Saviour.
Bus E, K.
There are lots of rock pools to explore at low tide in this uncrowded bay.

VAZON BAY Castel.
Bus E, K, F.
One of the best beaches for swimming, it is also popular with surfers.

CÔBO BAY Castel.
Bus F, G, H, K.
Probably the most popular beach on the island, with a windsurfing school and plenty of facilities for holiday-makers.

GRANDE HAVRE Vale.
Bus K, L, H.
Safe swimming and acres of sand at low tide. The best sunbathing is at the more sheltered Ladies Bay, towards the northern end.

L'ANCRESSE BAY Vale.
Bus J, K, L.
An almost circular sandy bay, popular with windsurfers and swimmers.

BORDEAUX HARBOUR Vale.
Bus J, K.
Good for swimming at high tide. Popular with divers and fishermen too.

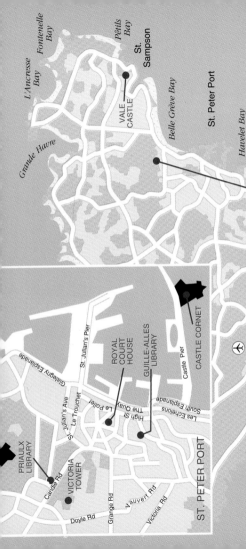

Buildings

CASTLE CORNET Castle Emplacement, St. Peter Port.
❑ 1030-1730 April-Oct. ❑ £2, child 75p.
Built by King John at the beginning of the 13thC, the castle is steeped in history and houses several interesting museums (including the Royal Guernsey Militia Museum) and exhibits.

ROYAL COURT HOUSE Manor Place, St. Peter Port.
❑ Court sessions Tue. & Thu. Public gallery 1000-1600. ❑ Free.
An opportunity to see the island's unique legal and administrative systems in action. Government meetings take place twice a month.

PRIAULX LIBRARY Candie Rd, St. Peter Port.
❑ 0930-1730 Mon.-Sat.
Beautiful old Candie House was converted to a library in 1887 and now houses a large collection of books on the history of the island.

VICTORIA TOWER Monument Rd, St. Peter Port.
❑ Get key from Fire Station control room across Arsenal Rd.
A castellated folly built in 1846 to commemorate a visit from Queen Victoria and used previously as a lookout station. There is a superb view from the top.

GUILLE-ALLES LIBRARY Market St, St. Peter Port.
❑ 0910-1700 Mon.-Wed., Fri.; 0910-1230 Thu.; 0910-1730 Sat.
There is a museum of Guernsey's natural history (see A-Z) on the top floor, and almost every book written about the island on the shelves.

CHATEAU DES MARAIS (Ivy Castle) Belle Grève Bay, St. Sampson. ❑ Unrestricted access. Bus J, K, L.
Recent excavations found 13thC coins around this medieval fortress which stands on a hill behind the bay.

VALE CASTLE Vale.
Bus K.
This once-imposing castle guards the northern side of St. Sampson's harbour. It is now in ruins but has played its part in Guernsey's history.

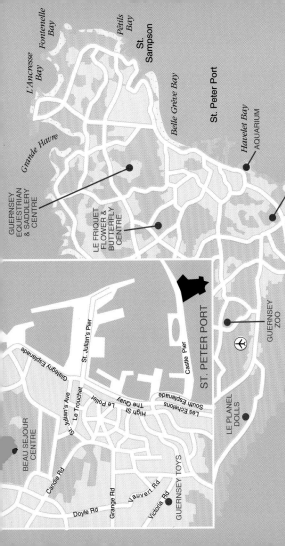

BEAU SEJOUR CENTRE Amhurst, St. Peter Port, tel: 728591.
❑ 0900-2300. Bus G. ❑ 50p. Water slides and pool £1.80, child £1.20;
roller-skating rink £1, child 80p; cinema £3, child £2.
A large entertainments complex with lots to keep everyone occupied:
pool with giant slides, roller skating, crazy golf, cafeteria and cinema.

LE FRIQUET FLOWER & BUTTERFLY CENTRE Castel,
tel: 54378. ❑ 1000-1700 Mar.-Nov. Bus F. ❑ £1.50, child £1.
Main attraction is the lovely butterfly house but there is also an indoor
playground, mini-golf, skittles and croquet; licensed café and gift shop.

GUERNSEY ZOO La Villiaze, St. Andrew, tel: 39176.
❑ 1000-1800 April-Sep., 1000-1600 Oct.-Mar. Bus M. ❑ £1.35, child 95p.
Private zoo with small rare and endangered South American species.

LE PLANEL DOLLS rue de Planel, Torteval, tel: 64326.
❑ 0900-1700 summer. Bus C. ❑ Free.
Beautiful dolls of all sizes in handmade, traditional Guernsey costumes.

AQUARIUM Half a mile south of the bus station, La Valette.
❑ 0900-dusk April-Oct.; 1000-dusk Nov.-Mar. ❑ £1.60, child 80p.
Fortified tunnel converted to tanks for tropical and local, marine and
freshwater fish and shellfish. Amusement arcade.

MANOR RAILWAYS Sausmarez Manor, St. Martin.
❑ 1000-1700. Bus A, B. ❑ £1.75, child 80p.
Rides through the woods in trains pulled by scale steam and diesel
locomotives on this miniature railway. 00-gauge model railway too.

GUERNSEY EQUESTRIAN & SADDLERY CENTRE
Les Grandes Capelles, St. Sampson, tel: 25257. Bus H. ❑ £8 per hr.
Early-morning rides on the beach or in quiet country lanes.

GUERNSEY TOYS 25-27 Victoria Rd, St. Peter Port, tel: 723871.
❑ 0900-1300, 1400-1700 Mon.-Fri.
Soft toys of every shape and size made on the premises.

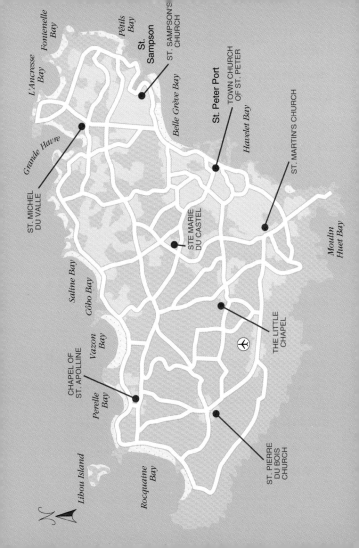

Churches

TOWN CHURCH OF ST. PETER Fountain St, St. Peter Port.
This squat granite church has seen many of the major events of the island's history, as its earliest stones were put in place by the Normans.

THE LITTLE CHAPEL Les Vauxbelets, St. Andrew.
Bus D, N, M.
Built by one of the monks from the nearby monastery, this tiny chapel is based on the shrine at Lourdes.

CHAPEL OF ST. APOLLINE Perelle, St. Saviour.
❑ Unrestricted access. Bus E, K.
The chapel and its frescoes have been carefully restored. St. Apolline is the patron saint of dentists and toothache sufferers!

ST. SAMPSON'S CHURCH St. Sampson.
Bus J.
St. Sampson, a Christian missionary, built an oratory here in the 6thC.

ST. MARTIN'S CHURCH St. Martin.
Bus A, B.
The main attraction here is La Gran'mère du Chimquiers, a stone figure dating back to the 6thC BC, and still venerated.

ST. MICHEL DU VALLE Vale.
Bus H.
Consecrated in 1117 and now believed to have been built on the site of a very early Christian community using old stones.

STE MARIE DU CASTEL Castel.
Bus E, F, N.
Built on the site of an ancient Viking fortress, there are striking frescoes and a 3000-year-old stone figure of a woman here.

ST. PIERRE DU BOIS CHURCH St. Pierre du Bois.
Bus C.
Stones from an earlier pagan sacred site are built into the walls here.

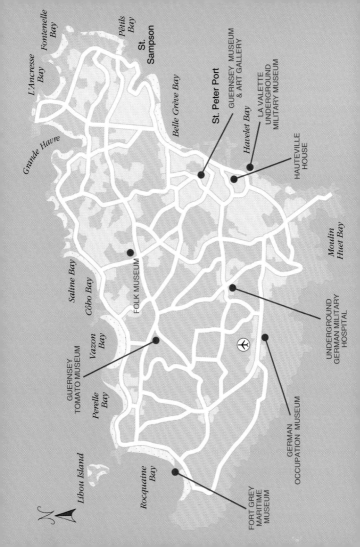

GUERNSEY MUSEUM & ART GALLERY Candie Rd, St. Peter Port. ❑ 1030-1730 summer, 1030-1630 winter. ❑ £1, child 40p.
Candie Gardens make a lovely setting for this new, award-winning museum with its displays on the history of the island and its people.

HAUTEVILLE HOUSE 38 Hauteville, St. Peter Port, tel: 21911. ❑ 1000-1130, 1400-1630 Mon.-Sat., April-Sep. ❑ £1.50, child 75p.
Writer Victor Hugo lived and worked here from 1855-70.

LA VALETTE UNDERGROUND MILITARY MUSEUM St. Peter Port, tel: 22300. ❑ 1000-dusk. ❑ £1.50, child 75p.
German tunnel complex houses exhibits from Guernsey's military history.

FOLK MUSEUM Saumarez Park, Castel. ❑ 1000-1730 Mar.-Oct. Bus F, N. ❑ £1.60, child 80p.
Farm buildings are used to house everyday items from the past.

GERMAN OCCUPATION MUSEUM Forest, tel: 38205. ❑ 1000-1700 April-Oct.; 1400-1630 Sun., Tue. & Thu., Nov.-Mar. Bus N, M, C. ❑ £1.50, child 75p.
*Displays, a life-size street and bunker rooms all tell the story of the German Occupation (see **A-Z**) of the island between 1940 and 1945.*

FORT GREY MARITIME MUSEUM St. Pierre du Bois. ❑ 1030-1230, 1330-1730 April-Oct. Bus C, K, D. ❑ 75p, child 30p.
Some of this coast's most dramatic shipwrecks are illustrated here.

GUERNSEY TOMATO MUSEUM Guernsey Village, Kings Mill, Castel, tel: 54389. ❑ 0900-2130 April-Nov. Bus E. ❑ £1.50, child 75p.
*A living museum showing the development of tomato growing over the past 100 years. Shop, restaurant and crafts on site (see **Drinks**).*

UNDERGROUND GERMAN MILITARY HOSPITAL St. Andrew. ❑ 1000-1200, 1400-1700 May-Sep.; 1400-1700 Tue., Thu. & Sun., April; 1400-1600 Tue., Thu. & Sun., Oct. Bus N. ❑ £1.50, child 75p.
*A cavernous and chilling reminder of the German Occupation (see **A-Z**).*

SCARLETT'S Ann's Place, St. Peter Port, tel: 713453.
❏ Licensed 2130-2345 Mon.-Sat. ❏ Members: Free Mon.-Thu., £2.50
Fri. & Sat. Non-members: Mon.-Thu. £2 (£3 after 2300), £4 Fri. & Sat.
Futuristic disco with good lighting and video screens, large seating areas and three bars. No jeans or trainers at weekends.

MARILYN'S Les Crouttes, St. Peter Port, tel: 27738.
❏ 2130-0100 Mon., Wed., Fri., Sat. ❏ £2.50 Mon., Wed., £4 Fri., Sat.
A popular disco with both islanders and visitors. The décor is smart and the atmosphere comfortable.

GOLDEN MONKEY Le Pollet, St. Peter Port, tel: 26755.
❏ 0930-1145. ❏ £2.50.
A relaxed meeting place which is apparently an amalgamation of a wine bar and dance venue.

DUKE OF RICHMOND HOTEL Cambridge Park, St. Peter Port.
Reservations, tel: 726221. ❏ Open to non-residents 1900-2300 Fri., Sat.
only. Jacket and tie required for men.
The candle-lit restaurant of this top hotel offers dancing to the music of the resident band during the summer.

SAVOY SUITE NIGHT CLUB Savoy Hotel, Glategny Esplanade,
St. Peter Port. ❏ 2045-2400 Mon.-Sat., 1900-2230 Sun.
Disco for 14 years +. Live band Wed.-Sat.; '50s and '60s music on Thu. Somewhat uninspiring décor but good atmosphere.

LONGFRIE HOTEL Longfrie, St. Pierre du Bois.
❏ Bar 1000-2300. Bus C.
Traditional Guernsey pub which livens up considerably in the evenings, with live music and discos in the summer.

NEW CARLTON CLUB Les Cornus Rd, St. Martin.
❏ 1930-2300 Mon.-Sat. Bus B, C. ❏ £2.50.
Ballroom dancing some nights, country-and-western singalong on Thu. Live entertainment Fri. and Sat. Advertised locally.

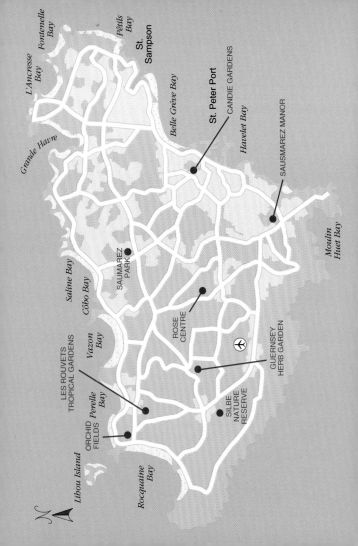

Parks & Gardens

CANDIE GARDENS St. Peter Port.
❏ 0800-dusk. ❏ Free.
Lovely park with fine views out over the harbour to the sea.

GUERNSEY HERB GARDEN Ashcroft Hotel, Sous l'Église,
St. Saviour, tel: 63862. ❏ 1000-1700 April-Oct. Bus D. ❏ Free.
Culinary, medicinal and aromatic herbs set out in traditional style. Shop selling fresh and dried herbs; licensed restaurant.

ROSE CENTRE Off Candie Rd, St. Andrew, tel: 36580.
❏ 0930-1700 March-Oct. Bus D, N. ❏ £1.50, child 50p.
Working indoor nursery reputed to be the best laid-out in Europe. Café.

LES ROUVETS TROPICAL GARDENS Perelle, St. Saviour,
tel: 63566. ❏ 1000-1700 summer. Bus E, C2. ❏ £1.20, child 60p.
Lakeside walk and tearoom complement greenhouses crammed with exotic flowers and trees – hibiscus, bananas, bougainvillea.

SAUMAREZ PARK Castel.
❏ 1000-1700. Bus F, N. ❏ Grounds free.
Formal gardens in front of the manor house and pleasant walks through the estate which hosts the annual North Show.

SAUSMAREZ MANOR St. Martin, tel: 38655.
❏ 1000-1800. Bus B. ❏ £1.75, child 80p.
Concerts are held here in the summer. Have a cream tea by the lake and wander among the exotic plants around this lovely old manor house.

ORCHID FIELDS rue des Vicheries, St. Pierre du Bois.
❏ Unrestricted access. Bus C1, C2.
Wetland habitat of some of Britain's rarest orchids; details from La Société Guernesiaise behind museum in Candie Gardens (see above).

SILBE NATURE RESERVE St. Pierre du Bois.
❏ Unrestricted access. Bus D1, D2.
Unspoilt area showing how Guernsey looked before development.

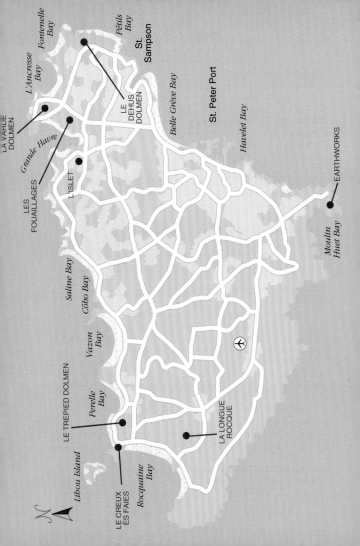

LE CREUX ÈS FAIES L'Erée, St. Pierre du Bois.
Bus D, E.
What was considered the legendary entrance to fairyland is in fact one of the best preserved of Guernsey's passage graves from 5000 years ago.

LA LONGUE ROCQUE St. Pierre du Bois.
Bus C.
The tallest of the remaining standing stones to be found on the island, this retained its fertility symbolism until very recently.

LES FOUAILLAGES Vale.
Bus K.
Recent excavations here have revealed the complicated rituals which surrounded the death and burial of early farming folk.

LA VARDE DOLMEN Vale.
Bus K.
At 36 ft long, this is the largest of the megalithic tombs in Guernsey.

LE DEHUS DOLMEN Vale.
Bus J.
The massive granite blocks which comprise the roof of this passage grave make it one of the most dramatic in western Europe.

L'ISLET St. Sampson.
Bus K, L.
A huge complex of stone circles within circles, a cist, or burial place, and the remains of a stone-lined tomb with antechambers.

LE TREPIED DOLMEN St. Saviour.
Bus K.
Witches were thought to worship at this 5000-year-old tomb in the 15thC.

EARTHWORKS Jerbourg Point, St. Martin.
Bus A.
There is evidence here of defensive earthworks dating back 3000 years.

Map labels

Fontenelle Bay
L'Ancresse Bay
Pétils Bay
St. Sampson
Belle Grève Bay
St. Peter Port
Grande Havre
Havelet Bay
FERMAIN TAVERN
LE CHALET COCKTAIL BAR
L'AUBERGE DIVETTE
Moulin Huet Bay

St. Peter Port inset

LACEY'S BAR & BISTRO
CHARLIE'S BAR
Glategny Esplanade
St. Julian's Pier
THE THOMAS DE LA RUE
St. Julian's Ave
Le Truchot
Le Pollet
The Quay
High St
South Esplanade
Les Echelons
Castle Pier
ST. PETER PORT
Candie Rd
TAYLOR'S WINE BAR
Grange Rd
Vauvert Rd
Victoria Rd
YACHT INN
Doyle Rd

CHARLIE'S BAR St. Julian's Ave, St. Peter Port.
❑ 1030-2200 Mon.-Sat.
This bar is smart and trendy, with live music several nights a week.

TAYLOR'S WINE BAR Town Arcade, St. Peter Port, tel: 25222.
❑ 1030-2200 Mon.-Sat.
A reasonable selection of wines is sold by the glass or bottle. Good food.

LACEY'S BAR & BISTRO St. George's Esplanade, St. Peter Port.
❑ 1030-2200 Mon.-Sat.
Part of the lovely old La Piette Hotel, on the seafront. Good beers and good food (lunch and supper only) served in a comfortable atmosphere.

THE THOMAS DE LA RUE Le Pollet, St. Peter Port.
❑ 1030-2200 Mon.-Sat.
Originally a printing works and now restored as a pub. Live music.

YACHT INN South Esplanade, St. Peter Port, tel: 20969.
❑ 1030-2200 Mon.-Sat.
One of the island's oldest inns, the Yacht looks a bit tatty from the outside but has a good atmosphere and serves tasty food (lunch and supper only).

FERMAIN TAVERN Fort Rd, St. Martin.
❑ 1030-2200 Mon.-Sat.
A good place for live music; top rock bands once a month, with a blues night every other Thu. Bar lunches and suppers.

L'AUBERGE DIVETTE Jerbourg, St. Martin.
❑ 1030-2200 Mon.-Sat.
*A Guernsey Brewery pub (see **Drinks**), L'Auberge Divette has a lovely garden which looks out over the sea to Herm, Jethou and Sark.*

LE CHALET COCKTAIL BAR Fermain Bay, St. Martin.
❑ 1030-2345.
At the back of the sun terrace perched above the beautiful Fermain Bay – a great spot for an ice cream or a sundowner or two.

DA NELLO'S 46 Le Pollet, St. Peter Port, tel: 21552.
❑ 1200-1400, 1830-2230. ❑ Moderate.
Fresh fish with an Italian flavour features in this atmospheric restaurant.

FLAVIO'S 56 Le Pollet, St. Peter Port, tel: 25055.
❑ 1200-1400, 1800-2230. ❑ Moderate.
Bistro with good-value seafood specialities and a French accent.

COURT'S WINE LODGE Le Marchant St, St. Peter Port, tel: 721782.
❑ 1130-1430, 1830-2230 Sun.-Fri. ❑ Moderate.
*Dark-wood panelling and intimate booths lend a stylish but unstuffy air.
Daily specials, vegetarian dishes and a wide-ranging wine list.*

ABSOLUTE END Longstore, St. Peter Port, tel: 23822.
❑ 1200-1400, 1900-2200 Mon.-Sat. ❑ Moderate.
*Converted from a little cottage on the outskirts of St. Peter Port, this
charming restaurant overlooks the sea and serves the freshest fish.*

CAFÉ D'ESCALIER 6 Tower Hill, St. Peter Port, tel: 710088.
❑ 1200-1400, 1900-2230 Mon.-Sat. ❑ Moderate.
*French-style restaurant in the oldest part of town offering classic game
and seafood as well as vegetarian dishes.*

LE GOUFFRE Forest, tel: 64121.
❑ 1200-1345 daily, 1900-2100 Mon.-Sat. Bus M, N. ❑ Moderate.
*Lovely setting for lunchtime barbecues; local seafood, house specials
and reasonably priced wines presented with a personal touch.*

CAFÉ DU MOULIN rue de Quanteraine, St. Pierre du Bois, tel:
65944. ❑ 1200-1400 Tue.-Sun., 1900-2200 Tue.-Sat. Bus C. ❑ Moderate.
*Converted from the granary of an old water mill near the west coast and
offering fine French cooking using fresh local produce.*

SHANI'S Fermain Hotel, Fort Rd, St. Martin's, tel: 35002.
❑ 1200-1400, 1730-2300. Bus B. ❑ Moderate.
Huge range of classic and unusual Indian dishes. Wonderful sweets.

PARTNERS Warwick House, Le Pollet, St. Peter Port, tel: 726624.
❑ 1200-1400 Mon.-Sat., 1800-2230 daily. ❑ Inexpensive.
Very popular with locals and visitors alike, so book in advance. Views over the harbour with fresh fish, steaks, pizzas and pasta.

ROCK GARDEN Lefebvre St, St. Peter Port.
❑ 1200-1430, 1800-2230 Mon.-Sat. ❑ Inexpensive.
Lively American-style hamburger bar with '60s memorabilia and music.

IL RUSTICO 44 Le Pollet, St. Peter Port, tel: 723246.
❑ 1200-1400, 1830-2230. ❑ Inexpensive.
Stylish but friendly Italian restaurant which serves well presented and generous helpings of both traditional favourites and house specials.

CAGNEY'S BISTRO 6 Contrée Mansell, St. Peter Port, tel: 27105.
❑ 1830-2230. ❑ Inexpensive.
A board features dishes of the day as well as the usual good selection of steaks, deep-pan pizzas, fresh fish and vegetarian specials.

FRIEND'S BISTRO North Esplanade, St. Peter Port, tel: 721503.
❑ 1200-1400, 1830-2200. ❑ Inexpensive.
Overlooks the harbour and offers seafood, pasta and vegetarian dishes.

ROCQUAINE BISTRO Pleinmont, Torteval, tel: 63149.
❑ 1030-2300. Bus C. ❑ Inexpensive.
Seafood restaurant and terrace overlooking the sea at Rocquaine Bay.

IMPERIAL HOTEL Pleinmont, Torteval, tel: 64044.
❑ 1200-1400, 1900-2115. Bus C. ❑ Inexpensive.
Famous for fresh shellfish from Rocquaine Bay, this is a good place for a traditional Sun. lunch after walk along the cliffs.

L'ISLET FISH & CHIP BAR Les Petites Mielles, St. Sampson, tel: 44654. ❑ 1130-1330, 1630-2330 Mon.-Sat. Bus H. ❑ Inexpensive.
Not only the best fish and chips but lamb-and-mint grills, fruit fritters, deep-fried prawns and squid with sweet-and-sour sauce.

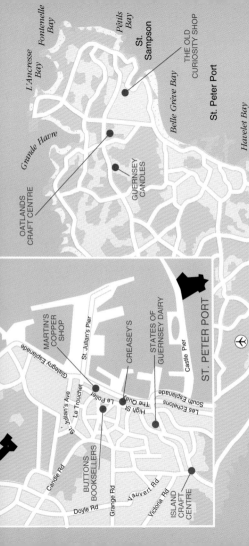

Fontenelle
Bay

Pêtils
Bay

St.
Sampson

THE OLD
CURIOSITY SHOP

L'Ancresse
Bay

Belle Grève Bay

St. Peter Port

Havelet Bay

Grande Havre

OATLANDS
CRAFT CENTRE

GUERNSEY
CANDLES

Moulin
Huet Bay

MARTIN'S
COPPER SHOP

Glategny Esplanade

St. Julian's Pier

CREASEY'S

STATES OF
GUERNSEY DAIRY

St. Julian's Ave

Le Pollet

Castle Pier

Le Truchot

High St
The Quay

ST. PETER PORT

Candie Rd

BUTTONS
BOOKSELLERS

Les Echelons

South Esplanade

Grange Rd

Vauvert Rd

Doyle Rd

Victoria Rd

ISLAND
CRAFT
CENTRE

STATES OF GUERNSEY DAIRY Market St, St. Peter Port.
❑ 0900-1700 Mon.-Sat.
The place to go for thick Guernsey cream and luscious milk shakes.

MARTIN'S COPPER SHOP 2-4 Le Pollet, St. Peter Port,
tel: 21725. ❑ 0930-1700 Mon.-Sat.
*The island's dairy herds used to be milked into handcrafted copper cans
and replicas of these make interesting souvenirs (see* **Cattle***).*

BUTTONS BOOKSELLERS Smith St, St. Peter Port.
❑ 0900-1730 Mon.-Sat.
*One of the best bookshops for local maps and books about the island's
wildlife, history, culture and daily life as well as holiday reading matter.*

ISLAND CRAFT CENTRE Trinity Sq., St. Peter Port.
❑ 0900-1700 Mon.-Sat.
*A good range of island crafts from independent producers, including
pottery, copperware, glass and knitwear. See* **Best Buys***.*

CREASEY'S High St, St. Peter Port.
❑ 0900-1700 Mon.-Sat.
*Guernsey's leading department store has a coffee shop on the top floor
and a Marks & Spencer section, including a food hall.*

OATLANDS CRAFT CENTRE Braye Rd, Vale.
❑ 0930-1630 summer. Bus L1, L2, N.
See the potters, jewellers, glassblowers and others at work before buying.

GUERNSEY CANDLES Les Petites Capelles, St. Sampson.
❑ 0900-2130 summer, 0900-1730 winter. Bus H1, H2.
Handcrafted candles of every shape, colour and description for sale.

THE OLD CURIOSITY SHOP Commercial Rd, St. Sampson,
tel: 45324. ❑ 0930-1700 Tue., Wed., Fri.-Sun. Bus J, N.
*A good place to look for old porcelain, sepia postcards and photographs,
Victorian jewellery, books, coins and silverware.*

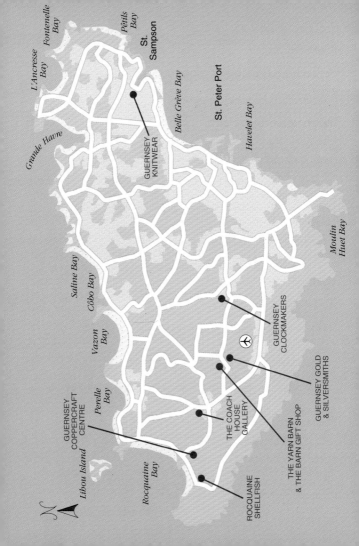

L'Ancresse Bay
Fontenelle Bay
Pêtils Bay
St. Sampson
Belle Grève Bay
St. Peter Port
Havelet Bay
Grande Havre
Moulin Huet Bay
Saline Bay
Côbo Bay
Vazon Bay
Perelle Bay
Rocquaine Bay
Libou Island

GUERNSEY KNITWEAR

GUERNSEY CLOCKMAKERS

GUERNSEY GOLD & SILVERSMITHS

GUERNSEY COPPERCRAFT CENTRE

THE COACH HOUSE GALLERY

THE YARN BARN & THE BARN GIFT SHOP

ROCQUAINE SHELLFISH

GUERNSEY KNITWEAR 6 The Bridge, St. Sampson, tel: 44487.
❑ 0930-1730 Mon.-Sat. Bus J, K, N.
Traditional island knitwear still produced to 'parish' designs; hard-wearing and workmanlike but also stylish. See **Best Buys**.

GUERNSEY CLOCKMAKERS Les Vauxbelets (behind The Little Chapel), St. Andrew's. ❑ 0800-1700. Bus D1, D2.
Standing in a lane is this intriguing workshop and showroom selling antique and new clocks, barometers and novelties.

GUERNSEY COPPERCRAFT CENTRE Rocquaine, St. Pierre du Bois, tel: 65112. ❑ 0930-1730. Bus C1, C2.
Another centre selling copper milk cans as well as brasswork and other goods made to order. Restaurant and licensed bar.

THE COACH HOUSE GALLERY Les Islets, St. Pierre du Bois, tel: 65339. ❑ 1100-1730. Bus C1, C2.
These converted farm buildings make a good backdrop to the sculpture, paintings, etchings, pottery and prints on sale here.

ROCQUAINE SHELLFISH Rocquaine Bay, St. Pierre du Bois.
❑ 0800-1800. Bus C.
The name says it all – oysters (a real bargain at £1.80 for six!) and ormers (see **Food***), live or dressed crab and lobster, and mussels, together with ormer shell jewellery, all for sale.*

GUERNSEY GOLD & SILVERSMITHS Le Gron, St. Saviour, tel: 64321. ❑ 0900-1700 Mon.-Sat. Bus D.
There is usually a demonstration of this delicate craft at 1045 each morning. You can purchase the results at the workshops and showroom.

THE YARN BARN & THE BARN GIFT SHOP
Bruce Russell Complex, Le Gron, St. Saviour, tel: 64321.
❑ 0900-1700 Mon.-Sat. Bus B.
Traditional Guernseys (see **Best Buys***) and exclusive mohair knitwear, with island souvenirs of toys, local perfume, pressed flowers and pottery.*

Mouisonnière Beach

Oyster Point

SHELL BEACH

Shell Bay

The Bear's Beach

ROBERT'S CROSS

CATTLE STALL

CHAPEL OF ST. TUGUAL

BELVOIR BAY

Spine Rd.

MANOR HOUSE & TOWER

Herm Harbour

The Drive

White House Hotel

THE PRISON

The Blue Lagoon

Puffin Bay

Bishop's Cove

N

What to See

THE PRISON By the White House Hotel.
❏ Unrestricted access.
Built in 1826 of Herm granite, this tiny, circular, windowless building looks more like a dovecote and is thought to be the world's smallest gaol.

SHELL BEACH Northeast coast.
❏ Unrestricted access.
A remarkable beach made up of millions of shells, many known only in the Gulf of Mexico. The café sells guides to theories on their origins.

BELVOIR BAY Directly across the island from the harbour.
❏ Unrestricted access.
A small, sheltered bay which is a suntrap. The conical rock offshore is called Caquorobert, after the helmet of Robert, Duke of Normandy.

MANOR HOUSE & TOWER Right in the middle of the island.
❏ Private home of the tenant.
The 18thC manor house was embellished in 1867 by tenant Colonel Fielden, who raised funds by smuggling brandy from France to England. The tower was built by his successor, Prince Blucher von Wahlstatt.

CHAPEL OF ST. TUGUAL Next to the Manor House.
❏ Unrestricted access.
Built in the 11thC to replace a chapel lost to the sea between Jethou and Herm; there are still regular services here. The belfry stands separately.

CATTLE STALL By the Manor House.
❏ Unrestricted access.
Oxen were used to haul granite when Herm exported stone and they were shod to protect their hooves. This stall held them upright while the farrier worked on each hoof in turn.

ROBERT'S CROSS On the southern edge of The Common.
❏ Unrestricted access.
The remains of a 16-ft-long passage grave are another reminder that pre-historic man laid claim to these 'heights' several thousand years ago.

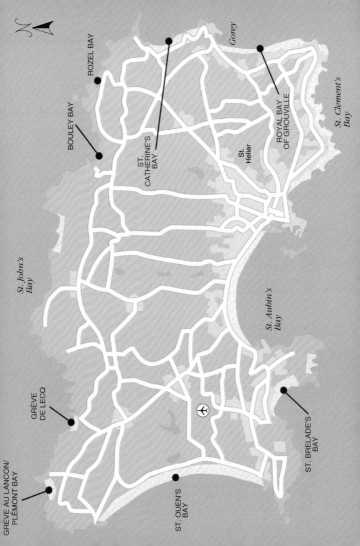

ST. OUEN'S BAY St. Ouen and St. Peter.
Bus 12A.
Five miles of beach and great surf, backed by dunes and nature reserves.

ST. BRELADE'S BAY St. Brelade.
Bus 12.
Sheltered beach popular for sunbathing and windsurfing. Good facilities.

ROYAL BAY OF GROUVILLE Grouville.
Bus 1/A, 2.
This beach lost millions of tons of sand to fortifications in the last war, but it is still ideal for families and has lovely views to Mont Orgueil.

ST. CATHERINE'S BAY St. Martin.
Bus 2.
Three quarters of a mile of breakwater protects this bay which includes Anne Port, sandy and good for swimming, Belval to the north and Archirondel, popular with locals.

ROZEL BAY Trinity and St. Martin.
Bus 3/B.
Pebbly but pretty, with lots of cafés and restaurants and lovely scenery.

BOULEY BAY Trinity.
Bus 4.
Shingle and deep water make this the ideal place for the local diving school, and nearby restaurants make the most of local crab and lobster.

GRÈVE DE LECQ St. Mary.
Bus 7B, 8.
Sandy and sheltered beach with rock outcrops.

GRÈVE AU LANCON/PLÉMONT BAY St. Ouen.
Bus 9/A.
*Half a mile of sandy beach at low water with interesting caves at western end, but beware the speed of the incoming tide (see **Tides & Currents**).*

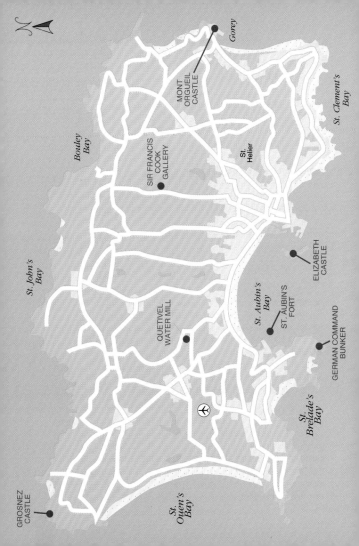

ELIZABETH CASTLE St. Helier, tel: 23971.
Walk at low tide across the causeway or take the ferry from West Park.
❑ 0930-1800 mid Mar.-end Oct. ❑ £1.20, child 75p.
Built in the 16thC and named after Elizabeth I by Sir Walter Raleigh.
There is an introductory exhibition, several museums and a shop.

GROSNEZ CASTLE Les Landes, St. Ouen.
❑ Unrestricted access. Bus 12A and walk.
Grosnez's massive granite walls are six ft thick and were probably built
in the 14thC as part of a series of defences against the French.

MONT ORGUEIL CASTLE Gorey, St. Martin, tel: 53292.
❑ 0930-1800 April-Oct. Bus 1/A, 2. ❑ £1.20, child 60p.
Mainly medieval but with a complicated history. You will need to follow
the signposts, exhibitions and tableaux to get the full picture.

ST. AUBIN'S FORT St. Aubin, St. Brelade.
❑ Unrestricted access. Bus 12/A, 15, 16 and walk at low tide.
Built to defend the town when Henry VIII was on the throne, it was last
*rebuilt by the Germans in World War II (see **German Occupation**).*

GERMAN COMMAND BUNKER Noirmont Point, St. Brelade,
tel: 82089. ❑ 1900-2130 Thu., June-Aug.
Spooky evening visits only are available to this large underground
bunker.

QUETIVEL WATER MILL St. Peter's Valley, St. Peter, tel: 83193.
❑ 1000-1600 Tue.-Thu., May-Oct. Bus 8. ❑ £1, child 20p.
Restored by the National Trust of Jersey, this is the last of some 40 water
mills which ground grain for the islanders from the earliest times. Others
in the area included Tesson, La Hague and Gigoulande.

SIR FRANCIS COOK GALLERY rue de Trinité, Augres, Trinity, tel:
63333. ❑ 1400-1700 Mon.-Sun. during exhibitions only. Bus 4. ❑ Free.
An old Methodist chapel converted by the artist to house his paintings.
*Also hosts temporary exhibitions – see newspapers (see **A-Z**) for details.*

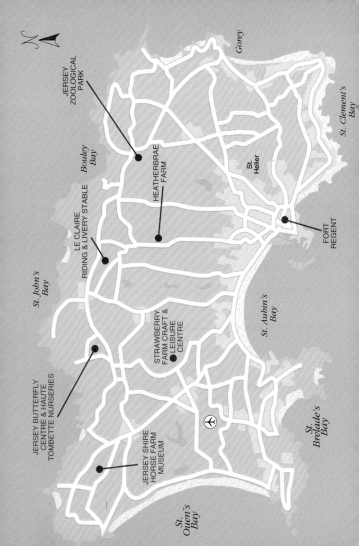

JERSEY ZOOLOGICAL PARK

HEATHERBRAE FARM

LE CLAIRE RIDING & LIVERY STABLE

JERSEY BUTTERFLY CENTRE & HAUTE TOMBETTE NURSERIES

STRAWBERRY FARM CRAFT & LEISURE CENTRE

JERSEY SHIRE HORSE FARM MUSEUM

FORT REGENT

St. Helier

Gorey

St. Clement's Bay

St. Aubin's Bay

St. Brelade's Bay

St. Ouen's Bay

St. John's Bay

Bouley Bay

FORT REGENT St. Helier, tel: 73000.
❏ 1000-2200 summer; 1000-1800 winter. ❏ £3; £4 including funfair.
Built originally as a fortress against Napoleon and now a huge leisure and entertainment complex offering live shows and displays to keep the whole family amused for hours. Reached by cable car from Snow Hill.

JERSEY SHIRE HORSE FARM MUSEUM Route de Trodez,
St. Ouen, tel: 82372. ❏ 1000-1730 Sun.-Fri., April-Nov. Bus 9A.
❏ £2.50, child £1.50.
Shires and Shetlands, pets corner, wagon rides and good farmhouse food.

JERSEY ZOOLOGICAL PARK Les Augres Manor, Trinity, tel:
64666. Bus 3/A/B. ❏ 1000-1800; dusk in winter. ❏ £3.50, child £2.
Gerald Durrell's world-famous headquarters of the Jersey Wildlife Preservation Trust. Rare animals and exotic birds in 25-acre landscaped park.

STRAWBERRY FARM CRAFT & LEISURE CENTRE
St. Peter's Valley, St. Peter. ❏ 1000-1730 Easter-end Oct. Bus 8. ❏ Free.
Children's playground with bouncy castle, pets corner, model village; potters and glassblowers at work. Strawberry cream teas for sale.

JERSEY BUTTERFLY CENTRE & HAUTE TOMBETTE NURSERIES Haute Tombette, St. Mary, tel: 81707.
❏ 0900-1800 mid Mar.-Nov. Bus 7. ❏ £2, child £1.60.
Rare tropical and exotic butterflies fly freely in a re-creation of their natural habitat alongside the carnation nursery. Gift shop and café.

LE CLAIRE RIDING & LIVERY STABLE St. John, tel: 62823.
Bus 5, 6. ❏ Hacking £8 per hr, £5 per half hr.
Lots of ponies suitable for taking children on the accompanied rides through some of Jersey's prettiest countryside.

HEATHERBRAE FARM St. John.
❏ 1430-1730 Mon.-Sat., May-Sep. Bus 5. ❏ Admission charge.
Meet the lovely Jersey cows and learn about milk production on a modern working dairy farm.

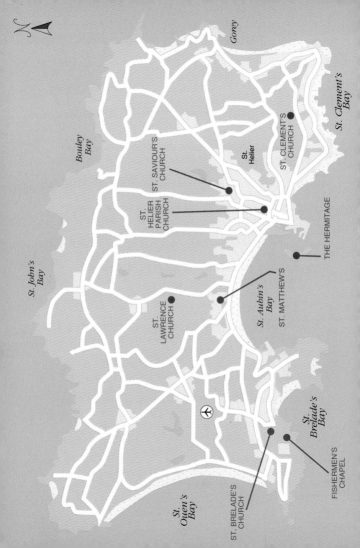

Churches

ST. HELIER PARISH CHURCH Church St, St. Helier.
*Named after the hermit St. Helier. This is the burial place of Major
Peirson who died defending the island from the French in 1781.*

THE HERMITAGE St. Helier.
Walk at low tide along the causeway to Elizabeth Castle.
*12thC chapel built on the site of St. Helier's hermitage, a small cave
where he lived for many years.*

ST. BRELADE'S CHURCH St. Brelade's Bay, St. Brelade.
Bus 12.
*Perhaps on the site of St. Brendan's (St. Brelade) first chapel, right by the
sea and built of rocks from the shore. Parts date back to the 12thC.*

FISHERMEN'S CHAPEL St. Brelade's Bay, St. Brelade.
Bus 12.
Medieval murals here are said to change with weather, warning of storms.

ST. MATTHEW'S (The Glass Church), Millbrook, St. Lawrence.
❏ 0900-1800 Mon.-Fri. (dusk in winter), 0900-1300 Sat. Bus 7, 8.
*Lalique glass font, altar rail, cross and pillars commissioned by the
widow of Baron Trent as a memorial to him.*

ST. SAVIOUR'S CHURCH St. Saviour.
Bus 3B.
12thC church known for lovely stained glass and Lillie Langtry's grave.

ST. CLEMENT'S CHURCH St. Clement.
Bus 1A.
*Beautiful 15thC frescoes depicting St. Michael and St. Margaret with the
Dragon, hunting scenes, and the martyr St. Barbara.*

ST. LAWRENCE CHURCH St. Lawrence.
Bus 7/B.
*Ancient gravestones built into the walls and an engraved Celtic granite
pillar dating back to AD 600 make this church worth a visit.*

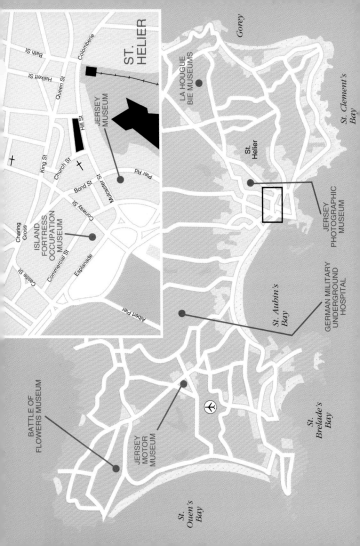

ST. HELIER

JERSEY MUSEUM

ISLAND FORTRESS OCCUPATION MUSEUM

Bath St
Halkett St
Queen St
Colomberie
Hill St
King St
Church St
Bond St
Conway St
Minden St
Pier Rd
Charing Cross
Castle St
Commercial St
Esplanade
Albert Pier

Gorey

LA HOUGUE BIE MUSEUMS

St. Helier

St. Clement's Bay

JERSEY PHOTOGRAPHIC MUSEUM

St. Aubin's Bay

GERMAN MILITARY UNDERGROUND HOSPITAL

BATTLE OF FLOWERS MUSEUM

JERSEY MOTOR MUSEUM

St. Ouen's Bay

St. Brelade's Bay

JERSEY MUSEUM 9 Pier Rd, St. Helier, tel: 30511.
❑ 1000-1700 Mon.-Sat. ❑ £1.20, child over 10 60p.
Local history from Neolithic times. Diverse displays feature Victorian dress, Lillie Langtry (see A-Z) and the German Occupation (see A-Z).

JERSEY PHOTOGRAPHIC MUSEUM Hotel de France,
St. Saviour's Rd, St. Helier, tel: 73102. ❑ 0900-1730 Mon.-Fri.,
0900-1230 Sat. Bus 3B. ❑ Free.
Frequently changed exhibitions of historical and contemporary photographs together with collections of cameras and other equipment.

ISLAND FORTRESS OCCUPATION MUSEUM 9 Esplanade,
St. Helier, tel: 34306. ❑ 0930-2230 Mar.-Oct. ❑ Admission charge.
*Everyday reminders of the Nazi Occupation with uniforms, documents, weapons and vehicles, plus a 40-min video. See **German Occupation**.*

BATTLE OF FLOWERS MUSEUM La Robeline, Mont des
Corvées, St. Ouen, tel: 82408. ❑ 1000-1700 Easter-Dec. Bus 9, 12A.
❑ £1.25, child 60p.
Displays of floats from the famous Battle of Flowers (see A-Z).

GERMAN MILITARY UNDERGROUND HOSPITAL Meadow
Bank, St. Peter, tel: 63442. ❑ 0930-1730 Mar.-Nov.; 1200-1700 Thu.,
1400-1700 Sun., Dec.-Feb. Bus 8. ❑ £3.30, child £1.50.
*Huge underground caverns excavated during World War II by prisoners of war, with explanatory audio-visual display. See **German Occupation**.*

JERSEY MOTOR MUSEUM St. Peter's Village, St. Peter,
tel: 82966. ❑ 1000-1700 Mar.-Nov. Bus 9/A. ❑ £1.30, child 70p.
Veteran and vintage cars, motorcycles, military vehicles, aero engines and a display relating to the defunct Jersey steam railway.

LA HOUGUE BIE MUSEUMS Grouville, tel: 53823.
❑ 1000-1630 Mar.-Oct. Bus 3A. ❑ £1.20, child 60p.
Site of fine Neolithic tomb, World War II bunker and museums of geology, archaeology, agriculture, Jersey steam railway and the Occupation.

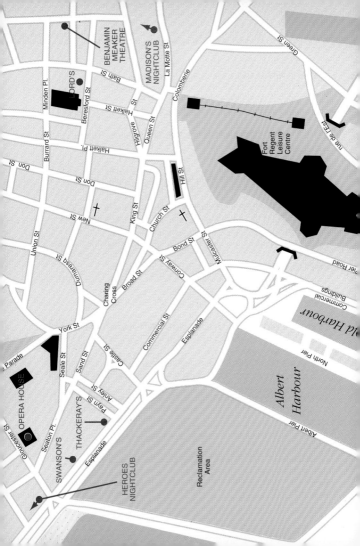

SWANSON'S Esplanade, St. Helier, tel: 58046.
❏ 1900-2345. ❏ £5.
Large and attractive bar with nightly cabaret entertainment and floor show in main season. Smart dress is preferred.

THACKERAY'S Esplanade, St. Helier, tel: 79023.
❏ 2100-0100. ❏ £2 weekdays, £3 Fri. & Sat., £2.50 Sun.
Jersey's best and most sophisticated disco, with videos and good lighting. Crowded with the money-making yuppie set.

LORD'S Beresford St, St. Helier, tel: 22921.
❏ 2100-0100. ❏ £2 Mon.-Thu., £3 Fri. & Sat.
Long-established and recently refurbished disco which is quite small but has excellent sound and lighting. No jeans at weekends.

MADISON'S NIGHTCLUB Lido de France, St. Saviour's Rd, St. Helier, tel: 73018. ❏ £2 Mon.-Wed., £2.50 Thu., Fri., £3 Sat.
With spectacular lighting, three bars and a good atmosphere, this disco is often full but never overcrowded, even at the height of the season.

HEROES NIGHTCLUB West Park, St. Helier, tel: 25521.
❏ 2100-0100 Mon.-Sat. ❏ £2.50 Mon.-Thu.; £3.50 Fri. & Sat.
❏ Under-18s disco 1930-2300. ❏ £2.50.
Popular nightspot for the younger element, with occasional discos for under 18s.

OPERA HOUSE Gloucester St, St. Helier, tel: 22165.
*Jersey's main traditional theatre presents touring theatre companies, concerts, pantomimes and, of course, the occasional opera. Details of performances can be found in the local press (see **Newspapers**).*

BENJAMIN MEAKER THEATRE Jersey Arts Centre, St. Helier, tel: 73767. ❏ Box office 1200-1400 Mon.-Fri., 1000-1400 Sat. and 30 min before each performance.
250-seat theatre featuring amateur and professional productions throughout the year; with a gallery and attractive bar and restaurant area.

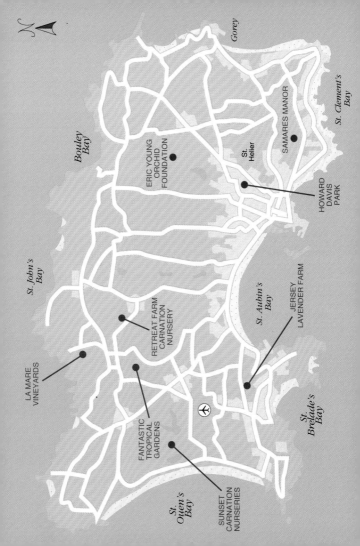

Parks & Gardens

HOWARD DAVIS PARK St. Saviour.
❏ 0700-dusk. Bus 2. ❏ Free.
Listen to music on summer evenings in this beautiful and spacious park.

LA MARE VINEYARDS Elms Farm, St. Mary, tel: 81178.
❏ 1000-1700 Mon.-Fri., May-Oct. Bus 7/B. ❏ £1.85, child 65p.
Vineyard, cider press, displays and produce for sale. Tea garden.

JERSEY LAVENDER FARM rue du Pont Marquet, St. Brelade, tel:
42933. ❏ 1000-1700 Mon.-Sat., May-Sep. Bus 15. ❏ £1.50, child free.
*Woodlands, herb garden, perfume distillery and some seven acres of
lavender which is stunning to the senses at harvest time.*

ERIC YOUNG ORCHID FOUNDATION Victoria Village, Trinity,
tel: 61963. ❏ 1000-1600 Thu.-Sat. Bus 21. ❏ £2, child £1.
World-renowned collection of these extraordinary flowers.

RETREAT FARM CARNATION NURSERY St. Lawrence,
tel: 65665. ❏ 0900-1730 summer; 0900-1700 Mon.-Fri., 0900-1300
Sat., winter. Bus 7. ❏ Free.
*Huge area of glasshouses with year-round colour; also aviary, café and
gift shop where you can buy cuttings and post flowers abroad.*

SUNSET CARNATION NURSERIES Val de la Mare, St. Ouen,
tel: 82090. ❏ 1000-1700 Mar.-Oct.; 1000-1630 Mon.-Fri., Nov.-Feb.
Bus 12A. ❏ Free.
*Carnations, gerberas and hanging strawberries are under glass, with
tropical gardens, a passion-flower maze, trout pool and aviary outside.*

SAMARES MANOR La Grande Route de St. Clement, St. Clement,
tel: 70551. ❏ 1000-1700 April-Oct. Bus 19. ❏ £2, child 80p.
Collection of exotic plants in beautiful manor grounds. Tea garden, shop.

FANTASTIC TROPICAL GARDENS St. Peter's Valley, St. Peter,
tel: 81585. ❏ 0930-1730 Mar.-Nov. Bus 8. ❏ £3.50, child £1.75.
Gardens planted in the themes of six countries, from four continents.

Fantastic Tropical Gardens, Jersey

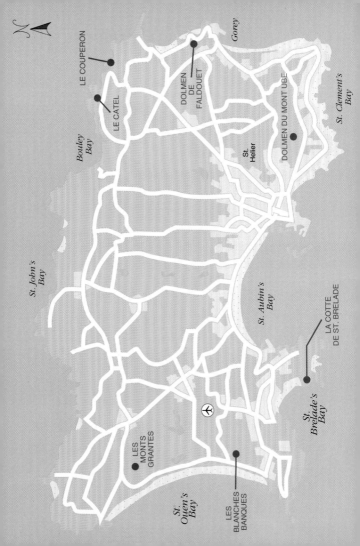

Prehistoric Sites

DOLMEN DE FALDOUET St. Martin.
❏ Unrestricted access. Bus 1/A to Gorey and walk.
*Excavated remains from this passage grave are on display at the Jersey Museum (see **JERSEY-MUSEUMS**). The capstone is said to weigh 24 tons.*

LE COUPERON St. Martin.
❏ Unrestricted access. Bus 3/B and walk east along coast.
A long, rectangular cist, or burial place, made up of two lines of stones, very similar to many in neighbouring Brittany.

DOLMEN DU MONT UBE St. Clement.
❏ Unrestricted access. Bus 1A and walk up hill.
*Another passage grave which is one of the oldest on the island, built by the first farmers to reach Jersey, some 4000 years ago. There are good views of Samares Manor (see **JERSEY-PARKS & GARDENS**) from here.*

LES MONTS GRANTES St. Ouen.
❏ Unrestricted access. Bus 12A to Kemp Tower and walk.
A well preserved passage grave, originally excavated in 1912, when the skeletons of seven adults and a child were removed.

LE CATEL Trinity.
❏ Unrestricted access. Bus 3/B to Rozel and walk west.
An earthwork dating back to the Iron Age but probably used by the Romans and possibly the Vikings, to judge from coins found here.

LES BLANCHES BANQUES St. Brelade.
❏ Unrestricted access. Bus 12A to Les Brayes and walk.
Dramatic standing stones known as the Great, Little and Broken Menhirs are set in the sand dunes behind the beach.

LA COTTE DE ST. BRELADE St. Brelade.
❏ Unrestricted access. Bus 16.
One of the finest Palaeolithic sites in Europe, which has yielded thousands of stone tools and bones dating back 70,000 years.

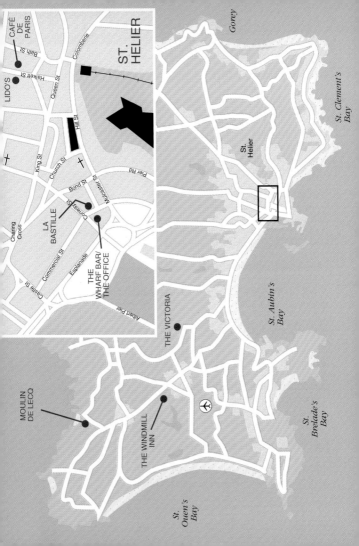

LIDO'S 4-6 Market St, off Halkett St, St. Helier, tel: 22358.
❑ 1100-2200 Mon.-Sat.
Crowded 1960s-style wine bar with freshly cooked daily specials offering excellent value for money.

THE WHARF BAR Wharf St, St. Helier, tel: 78644.
❑ 1000-2200 Mon.-Sat., 1100-1300, 1630-2200 Sun.
Above-average pub grub (lunch only) and good, well-kept local beer.

LA BASTILLE 4 Wharf St, St. Helier, tel: 74059.
❑ 1030-2200 Mon.-Sat.
Well-established wine bar with extensive choice of wine and champagne; menu includes hot and cold dishes, and oysters!

THE OFFICE Wharf St, St. Helier, tel: 23687.
❑ 0900-2200 Mon.-Sat., 1100-1300, 1630-2200 Sun.
A comfortable, well-run pub with a pleasant atmosphere and interesting food (lunch only) at reasonable prices.

CAFÉ DE PARIS Halkett St, St. Helier.
❑ 0900-2200 Mon.-Sat., 1100-1300, 1630-2200 Sun.
An interesting building right in the heart of town and offering good bar food as well as fine local beers.

MOULIN DE LECQ Grève de Lecq, St. Ouen.
❑ 1000-2200 Mon.-Sat., 1100-1300, 1630-2200 Sun.
This inn was formerly the parish water mill and you can still see some of the ancient grinding gear.

THE VICTORIA St. Peter's Valley, St. Peter.
❑ 1000-2200 Mon.-Sat., 1100-1300, 1630-2200 Sun.
Pleasant tavern in a building which is typical of fine Jersey architecture.

THE WINDMILL INN St. Peter.
❑ 1000-2200 Mon.-Sat., 1100-1300, 1630-2200 Sun.
Atmospheric tavern built around a pretty old windmill. Fine local beer.

LITTLE GROVE HOTEL rue de Haut, St. Lawrence, tel: 25321.
❑ 1900-2200. ❑ Expensive.
Granite-walled country house where the cooking is exceptional in its originality and in its quality and presentation.

THE LOBSTER POT L'Etacq, St. Ouen, tel: 82888.
❑ 1000-2300. ❑ Expensive.
A famous restaurant specializing in Jersey seafood and continental gastronomy. With lounge bar and buffet salad bar.

THE MOORINGS Gorey Pier, St. Martin, tel: 53633.
❑ 1200-1400, 1800-2200. ❑ Moderate.
Expect a warm welcome at this well-respected restaurant where you might choose lamb carved from the trolley or fresh seafood.

GRANITE CORNER Rozel Harbour, St. Martin, tel: 63590.
❑ 1200-1400 Tue.-Sun., 1900-2200 Tue.-Sat. ❑ Moderate.
The French chef/patron has created a stylish French provincial restaurant.

TAJ MAHAL La Pulente, St. Ouen, tel: 44400.
❑ 1130-1430, 1730-2200. ❑ Moderate.
Overlooking St. Ouen's Bay, this is an outstanding spot for an Indian barbecue outside in summer or an excellent meal anytime.

RISTORANTE BAR ISOLA BELLA St. Aubin's Rd, First Tower, St. Helier, tel: 23427. ❑ 1130-1400, 1830-2200 Thu.-Tue. ❑ Moderate.
Family-owned Italian eatery serving home-made pasta and good wines.

MICHEL'S Mont les Vaux, St. Aubin, tel: 44043.
❑ 1200-1400 Thu.-Tue., 1800-2200 daily. ❑ Moderate.
A simple, friendly bistro run by a French chef and his Irish wife who provide well cooked food to suit a wide range of tastes.

SEASCALE Gorey Pier, St. Martin, tel: 54395.
❑ 1200-1430, 1800-2200. ❑ Moderate.
Service is rapid and pleasant in this small, harbourside seafood eatery.

BISTRO LE NORMAND 10-12 Beresford St, St. Helier, tel: 32522.
❑ 1200-1430 Mon.-Sat., 1830-2200 Tue.-Sat. ❑ Inexpensive.
Delightfully idiosyncratic bistro run by a French chef who is unlikely to produce a predictable menu. Interesting wine list.

ALBERT J. RAMSBOTTOM'S 90-92 Halkett Place, St. Helier, tel: 78772. ❑ 1130-1400 Mon.-Sat., 1700-2200 daily. ❑ Inexpensive.
Rapidly becoming an institution; come here for chunky chips, mushy peas and wonderfully light and crisp golden batter on fresh fish.

BILBO'S 8A Waterloo St, St. Helier, tel: 35367.
❑ 1100-2230 Mon.-Sat., 1100-1400 Sun. ❑ Inexpensive.
Non-stop videos form the background to fast food in generous portions.

TRATTORIA CENTRALE 9-11 Don St, St. Helier, tel: 76933.
❑ 1200-1400, 1800-2200 Mon.-Sat. ❑ Inexpensive.
Friendly trattoria offering a variety of pasta, charcoal grills and specials.

MONT ORGUEIL Gorey Hill, St. Martin, tel: 53291.
❑ 1130-1430, 1730-2130. ❑ Inexpensive.
Bustling and successful bistro above the harbour where you can get a full meal or just a snack. Interesting wine selection.

ARGILSTON VEGETARIAN RESTAURANT Mont Nicolle, St. Brelade, tel: 44027. ❑ 1100-1400, 1730-2130 Tue.-Sun. ❑ Inexpensive.
Boasts an imaginative menu which surpasses the usual nut-roast offering.

LE DAUPHIN St. Brelade's Bay, St. Brelade, tel: 41821.
❑ 1200-1400, 1830-2200 Mon., Wed.-Sat. ❑ Inexpensive.
Overlooking the beach, this pleasant restaurant creates the right kind of atmosphere for a casual night out.

BORSALINO ROCQUE La Rocque, Grouville, tel: 52111.
❑ 1200-1430, 1830-2200. ❑ Inexpensive.
Bar and restaurant with conservatory area; superb shellfish, imaginative menus and a respectable wine list.

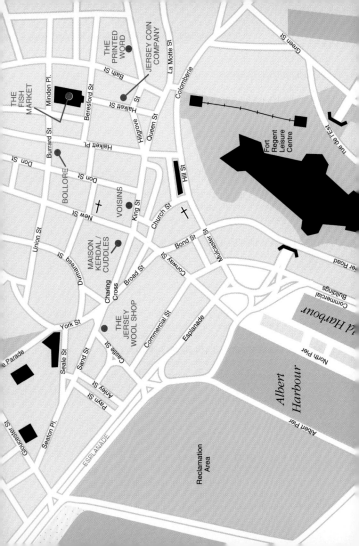

Shopping 1

THE FISH MARKET Beresford St, St. Helier.
❏ 0730-1300 Mon.-Sat.
The best time to come here is first thing in the morning, when the fresh catch is looking its best straight from the sea.

MAISON KERDAL 45 King St, St. Helier.
❏ 0930-1730 Mon.-Sat.
This is a pleasantly old-fashioned and atmospheric place to come to choose your cigars, brandy, vintage port and malt whisky.

CUDDLES 45 King St, St. Helier.
❏ 0900-1730 Mon.-Sat.
Every shape and size of furry animal – ideal for cuddly-toy collectors.

VOISINS King St, St. Helier, tel: 70511.
❏ 0900-1730 Mon.-Sat.
Department store with a particularly tempting ground-floor patisserie!

THE JERSEY WOOL SHOP 2 Charing Cross, St. Helier, tel: 20663.
❏ 0930-1730 Mon.-Sat.
*Traditional Jersey and Guernsey woollens (see **Best Buys**); Aran wool and clothes, tapestries, patterns and yarns from Europe, too.*

BOLLORE 14 Burrard St, St. Helier, tel: 37206.
❏ 0930-1730 Mon.-Sat.
An exotic selection of oriental goods, including silk kimonos, rosewood furniture and jade ornaments, as well as cloisonné ware.

JERSEY COIN COMPANY 26 Halkett St, St. Helier, tel: 25743.
❏ 0900-1700 Mon.-Sat.
Collectors will make a beeline for this coin and bullion dealer which also sells gold coins, rings and pendants.

THE PRINTED WORD 7 West's Centre, St. Helier, tel: 68524.
❏ 0900-1730 Mon.-Sat.
Bright bookshop well stocked with holiday reading, maps and guides.

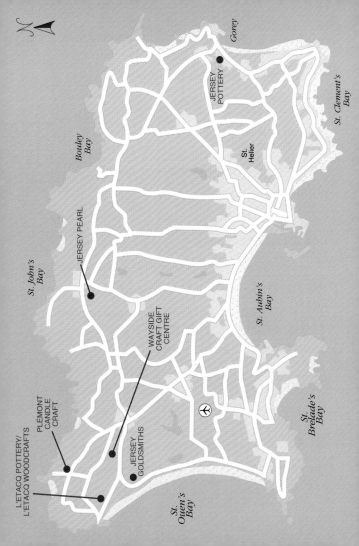

JERSEY POTTERY Gorey Village, Grouville, tel: 51119.
❑ 0900-1730 Mon.-Fri. Bus 1/A, 2.
Watch the potters at work before you buy in the pottery shop here or in Bond St, St. Helier. Café and restaurant.

L'ETACQ POTTERY L'Etacq, St. Ouen, tel: 82142.
❑ 0900-1730. Bus 12A. ❑ Free.
Beautifully coloured pottery decorated with fruit, flowers and vegetables.

PLÉMONT CANDLE CRAFT Portinfer, St. Ouen, tel: 82146.
❑ 0930-1730 Mar.-Sep.; 1000-1600 Mon.-Fri., Oct.-Feb. Bus 9. ❑ Free.
Handmade candles of every shape and colour, decorated and carved, are for sale from the cottage where they are made.

L'ETACQ WOODCRAFTS L'Etacq, St. Ouen, tel: 82142.
❑ 1000-1700 Mon.-Fri., 1000-1630 Sat., Sun. Easter-Oct.; 1030-1300, 1400-1630 Mon.-Sat., Nov.-Easter. Bus 12A.
Not only woodwork but carved cabbage stalks too! Exhibition and video as well as sales showroom and café (in summer). See **Best Buys***.*

JERSEY GOLDSMITHS Five Mile Rd, St. Ouen, tel: 82098.
❑ 1000-2200 Mon.-Fri., 1000-1730 Sat., May-Sep.; 1000-1730 Mon.-Sat., Oct.-April. Bus 12A. ❑ Free.
No VAT (Value-Added Tax) and low duty make jewellery a particular bargain in Jersey and here you can see craftsmen at work before you buy.

WAYSIDE CRAFT GIFT CENTRE Haut de Marais, St. Ouen.
❑ 0900-1700. Bus 9/A.
A good place to come to if you are looking for something made on the island to take home as a souvenir.

JERSEY PEARL rue des Issues, St. John, tel: 62137.
❑ 1000-2200 Mon.-Fri., 1000-1730 Sat., May-Sep.; 1000-1730 Mon.-Sat. Bus 5, 6. ❑ Free.
Another good spot for jewellery designed and made on the spot and well displayed in a spacious showroom.

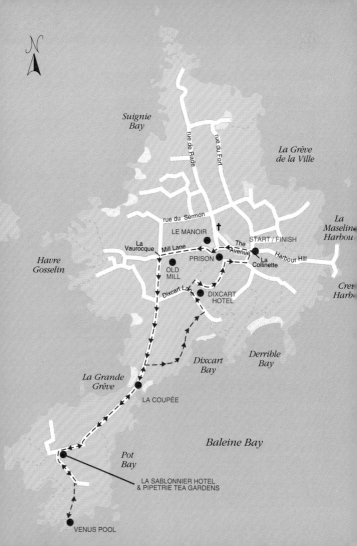

Walk

A three-and-a-half-mile walk through south Sark to Little Sark. Details of most of the attractions mentioned can be found in SARK-WHAT TO SEE.

There are a number of footpaths on Sark which are clearly marked on most maps and which will take you from the main routes to the extremities of the island. The way of life here is geared to walking and cycling, so there is no danger attached to walking on the loose-surfaced roads, except that they can be muddy in wet weather and dusty in the dry, so take appropriate footwear. Paths down to the beaches are very steep. Most directions on the island are given from the crossroads at the top of Harbour Hill which is known as La Collinette. There are two banks here as well as a horse-drawn carriage for hire, and it is as good a place as any to start your walk.

Set off westwards along The Avenue through the heart of downtown Sark, a motley collection of little stores, bicycle-hire and gift shops. The post office and the church are off to the right but on your left you'll come to the school and the prison. This little, barrel-roofed building was built in 1856 and contains two cells, still used occasionally for offenders.

On the other side of the road is Le Manoir, the 16thC home of the Seigneur before La Seigneurie was built. The Mill on your left is now a gift shop and the sails have gone but it was well placed at just about the highest point on the island to catch every wind. Turn left at the crossroads of La Vaurocque, and the roadway continues south for the next mile and a quarter. Along the way you will notice that each house hangs a little milk churn out for their daily delivery. There are ormer shells (see **Food**) set into the wall of Farmhouse Plaisance for decoration. As you reach the brow of the hill a wide view of the sea opens up on your left and you can see both Little Sark and the much smaller hump of L'Etac off to the south.

As you begin to drop down towards La Coupée there is a cannon set up off the road to your right, dating from around 1790 and placed here in 1983. La Coupée is the narrow causeway which links Sark with Little Sark. Halfway across there is a plaque which tells that 'In 1945 the roadway was rebuilt in concrete with handrails by German prisoner of war labour directed by 259 Field Company Royal Engineers'. Before

that it was sometimes necessary to crawl across on hands and knees if the weather was bad!

You are now on Little Sark and to mark your arrival, take a seat to the right above the road and look at the view. Below is La Grande Grève, at low water showing a spectacular stretch of sand reached by a precipitous path which starts at the Sark end of La Coupée; the Pilcher monument stands out on the headland beyond and the island of Brecqhou (see **A-Z**) just offshore. On clear days you can look across to Herm, Jethou and Guernsey.

Carry on along the tree-lined lane with cattle grazing on either side and you will come to La Sablonnier Hotel and Pipetrie Tea Gardens for a well-earned lunch or afternoon tea. This walk ends here but if you take the left-hand lane, after about 400 yd there is a footpath off to your right which will take you down through the old silver mines to Venus Pool, a huge rock pool which is left exposed at low tide and is a glorious place to swim.

Return by the same lane but after you cross La Coupée turn right onto the footpath opposite the old cannon and follow the coast path around to Dixcart Bay. This will give you a good view of Sark's east coast to the Hogsback and Derrible Bay and even across to France when the visibility is good. When you reach a stile into a rough lane turn left and you will come to the friendly Dixcart Hotel, which has good bar food. There is a footpath back to The Avenue just beyond Stocks Hotel next door.

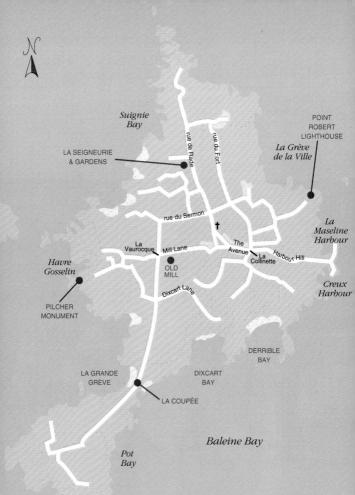

N

Suignie Bay

LA SEIGNEURIE & GARDENS

rue de Rade

rue du Fort

POINT ROBERT LIGHTHOUSE

La Grève de la Ville

rue du Sermon

La Maseline Harbour

La Vaurocque

Mill Lane

The Avenue

La Collinette

Harbour Hill

Havre Gosselin

OLD MILL

PILCHER MONUMENT

Dixcart Lane

Creux Harbour

DERRIBLE BAY

LA GRANDE GRÈVE

DIXCART BAY

LA COUPÉE

Baleine Bay

Pot Bay

What to See

DIXCART BAY/DERRIBLE BAY South Sark.

Dixcart Bay is the easiest beach on the island to get down to and is sheltered from all winds except southerlies. It has a good stretch of sand at low water. Neighbouring Derrible Bay is beautiful but is Sark's least accessible beach.

LA COUPÉE Between Sark and Little Sark.

❏ Unrestricted access.

La Coupée is a very narrow path perched on a ridge joining Sark to Little Sark. It is c.260 ft above sea level – not a place for vertigo sufferers!

LA GRANDE GRÈVE To the west of La Coupée (see above).

This beach seems unremarkable at half tide but produces a fine expanse of sand at low water. It is reached only by a very steep path.

LA SEIGNEURIE & GARDENS Northeast Sark.

❏ Gardens 1000-1700 Wed., Fri. & bank hol. House private property.

The home of the Seigneur, this is an imposing stone house built in 1730 and set in sheltered, wooded and walled gardens.

PILCHER MONUMENT West Sark.

❏ Unrestricted access.

A personal reminder of J. Pilcher who drowned in these treacherous waters on his way back to Guernsey in 1868, this stark granite obelisk is also a reminder of countless other victims of the sea.

OLD MILL Mill Lane.

❏ 0900-1700.

At 356 ft above sea level, the mill was placed so that its sails could catch every wind. It was built in 1571 and is now a gift shop, without sails!

POINT ROBERT LIGHTHOUSE East Sark.

❏ 1300-1700 summer. Tours only.

Built in 1912 to warn passing shipping of the island's rocky coast and to guide local fishermen home. There are around 146 steps down the cliff to the entrance and plenty more up into the tower itself.

Castle Cornet, Guernsey

Accidents & Breakdowns: If you are involved in a car accident on Jersey, inform a police officer and do not move your car without permission. In country areas you should inform the local *centenier* (see **Police**) – ask a local resident for the official's whereabouts. On Alderney and Guernsey, accidents involving personal injury or serious damage must be reported to the police within 24 hr. Minor accidents need not be reported provided the names and addresses of those involved are exchanged. See **Driving**, **Emergency Numbers**.

Moulin de Lecq, Jersey

Accommodation: Each of the islands operates a different grading system for accommodation. On Jersey there are First Register hotels, which are awarded between one and four 'suns', and Second Register hotels, which have between one and four 'diamonds'. Guesthouses are graded A, B or C and the overall standard is very high. On Guernsey hotels are graded locally using a crown symbol, ranging from one to five according to standards and amenities on offer. Registered hotels are approved by the tourist board but do not merit a crown. Guesthouses are graded by letter (A-D), as is self-catering accommodation. The majority of hotels on Alderney offer en-suite accommodation and there is a wide selection of guesthouses and self-catering property, too. Sark can only accommodate 500 guests in its few small hotels, so early booking is recommended. Herm has one hotel, the White House Hotel, tel: 22159; for self-catering cottages, tel: 22377. See **Camping & Caravanning, Tourist Information, Youth Hostels**.

Airports: Jersey Airport, tel: 46111, is four miles from St. Helier. Its facilities include car-hire desks, souvenir and duty-free shops, a restaurant, bar, newsagent and flower shop, as well as a helpful information desk. Left-luggage facilities may be suspended for security reasons. Bus 15 will take you to or from the town centre in about 15 min (95p). Guernsey Airport, tel: 37424, is three and a half miles from St. Peter Port and has a duty-free shop, café, flower shop and newsagent on site. There is a tourist information desk with an accommodation booking service. Bus C every 30 min will take you to town for 75p. Alderney Airport, tel: 822624, is only half a mile from St. Anne and is not on the summer bus route, though there are taxis (see **A-Z**) and local hotels provide transport. However, if your bags are not heavy it is only 10 minutes' walk to St. Anne!

Alderney: The most northerly of the Channel Islands, Alderney is just 60 miles from mainland Britain as well as being very close to France, at only eight miles from Cap de la Hague on Normandy's northwestern tip. It is the third-largest island in the group but is considerably smaller than Jersey and Guernsey, being about three and a half by one and a half miles. This makes it a very manageable place, small enough to explore thoroughly during a holiday but big enough to offer a variety of beaches, walks, scenery and facilities. On an island this small you will be greeting people like old friends within days of your arrival and it is impossible to get lost for long. The character of the land itself is very different from any of the other Channel Islands. Alderney is fairly flat, rising at its highest point to less than 300 ft above sea level and it can seem bleak and exposed when the wind gets up. Yet it is surprising how warm it can be in the lee of a rock, below a sand dune or in the shallowest of valleys. There are acres of white sand on the north coast at Braye, Saye, Arch and Corblets if the wind is blowing from the south or east; head for Longis or Telegraph Bays to avoid a wind from the west or north.

Inevitably, Alderney has its own individual history: the massive fortifications created in the mid 1800s, the abandonment of the island in the face of the German invasion, and the horrors of the concentration and forced-labour camps. Today it is home to some 2500 people, many of whom bear the names of their French forebears, who live quiet, unhurried lives away from the frenetic world of the mainland. Alderney will appeal if you enjoy this sense of island life, where you are inevitably aware of the elements, of the power of the sea and its gifts, of the birds that make it their home and the flowers that brave the winds. There are things to do on wet days but Alderney is primarily a place for self-sufficient visitors, interested in walking (see **A-Z**), birdwatching (see **A-Z**) or fishing (see **A-Z**). It is possible to fly in for the day from the other main islands but this is not cheap and the island is better appreciated as a holiday destination in its own right. On good summer days there are day trips from here by sea around the island, to the bird reserve of Burhou (see **A-Z**), the gannetries of Ortac and Les Etacs, and even to France. Remember that you are not that far from England, so wet-weather gear and warm clothing is essential at any time of the year, particularly on the water! See **ALDERNEY-WHAT TO SEE**.

How to get there – by air (from Southampton), tel: 0703-612829 or Aurigny Air Services, St. Anne, tel. 2886; from Jersey and Guernsey, Aurigny Air Services, Weighbridge, St. Helier, tel: 35733 or South Esplanade, St. Peter Port, tel: 23474.

Baby-sitters: Hotels and guesthouses will often offer a baby-listening service and will recommend reliable local baby-sitters. If you are on a self-catering or camping holiday look for advertisements in local newspapers (see **A-Z**) and in newsagents, or ask at the tourist board offices (see **Tourist Information**). Guernsey has several helpful organizations: Friends of the Family, tel: 47476; Guernsey Baby-sitting Group, tel: 23221; Sitter Service, tel: 53893. Alderney has a visitor hot-line which can offer advice, tel: 2994. See **Children**.

Banks: See **Currency, Money, Opening Times**.

Battle of Flowers: The first Battle of Flowers was first held on 9 Aug. 1902 to celebrate the coronation of Edward VII and since then it has become one of the island's major tourist events. It is held annually on the second Thu. in Aug. Floats completely covered in flowers process along Victoria Ave from West Park to rue du Glaet, St. Lawrence, where extravagant displays and exhibits fill an arena. The 'battle' element, in which the floats were stripped of the flowers which were then hurled by the competitors at the crowd, has been discontinued. The Battle of Flowers Museum at La Robeline gives a good idea of the scale of the festival if you don't happen to be on the island at the right time for the event itself (see **JERSEY-MUSEUMS**). A similar festival is held on Guernsey in Saumarez Park (see **Events**).

Best Buys: Apparently duty-free shopping can be a trap – don't imagine that you can buy anything you like and take it back to the UK without paying tax! There are bargains to be had, however, in some cosmetics, lighters and jewellery. There is no VAT (Value-Added Tax) charged in the Channel Islands. All the islands have craft centres where

quality pottery, wood carving, glass and other handmade souvenirs are for sale. In Jersey, a particular speciality is the carved stem of the giant cabbage, made into walking sticks and sold at L'Etacq Woodcrafts (see **JERSEY-SHOPPING 2**).

Guernsey's speciality is knitwear. Guernsey sweaters were knitted to a particular pattern in each parish so that drowned fishermen could be readily identified. Today the best ones are still the working version: strong, oiled wool with no side seams or elaborate patterns other than the definitive stitching around the shoulders and the hem. For traditional Guernseys, try Le Tricoteur, Pitronnerie Rd, St. Peter Port, tel: 26214. See **GUERNSEY-SHOPPING**, **JERSEY-SHOPPING**, **Markets**, **Shopping**.

Bicycle & Motorcycle Hire: All the islands are ideal for bicycles, being relatively small and never too hilly. Guernsey even has an Easter Festival of Cycling; for more information, contact Jenny Rhodes, La Palitole, Clos du Moulin, St. Martin's, tel: 35844.

Hire shops on the various islands are as follows:

Jersey – Hireride, St. John's Rd, St. Helier, tel: 31995/51405; Kingslea, The Esplanade, St. Helier, tel: 24777.

Guernsey – Moullins Cycle Shop, St. George's Esplanade, St. Peter Port, tel: 721581; The Cycle & Unipart Shop, The Bridge, St. Sampson's, tel: 49311; Perrio's, Chescot, Route Carre, L'Islet, St. Sampson's, tel: 45217; Galaad Cycle Hire, Hougue du Pommier, Castel, tel: 53322; Wheel House Cycle Hire, Lindale, rue Maze, St. Martin's, tel: 36815; West Coast Cycles, Les Tamaris, Portinfer Lane, Vale, tel: 53654.

Alderney – Pedal Power, Les Rocquettes, tel: 2286; J. B. Cycle Hire, Albert Mews, tel: 2294; Da Salvatore's Cycle Hire, tel: 2689; Le Banquage Cycle Hire, tel: 2000.

Sark – Jackson's Cycle Hire, The Avenue (0630-1730 Mon.-Sat., summer; by appointment in winter).

Motorcycles can also be hired by the day or week, but you must be 18 years old, have a full driving licence, and both pillion and driver must wear helmets. For motorcycle hire on Jersey, see the bicycle-hire listings above. On Guernsey, Millard & Co. Ltd, Victoria Rd, St. Peter Port, tel: 720777, have motorcycles for hire. For hire on Alderney, see **Car Hire**. Sark does not allow motorcycles. See **Driving**.

Bird-watching: There is a huge variety of habitats on offer throughout the islands, from marsh to heathland, from cliffs to sand and mud flats, from saltwater to freshwater, so a birdwatcher is unlikely to be short of things to see. Some birds, such as the Dartford warbler and the marsh harrier which are rare on the mainland, are common here. The Channel Islands are well situated on the spring (Mar.-May) and autumn (Aug.-Nov.) migratory routes of birds flying between their breeding grounds in the north and their southern winter habitats.

But perhaps the most impressive sights ornithologically are the gannet colonies off Alderney. These magnificent sea birds have a few exclusive nesting sites around the coast of Britain, yet Alderney boasts two: the Ortac, with around 1000 nesting pairs, and Les Etacs, with around 2000 pairs. Boat trips around these rocks can be arranged locally and are very rewarding: gannets diving into the sea, seen at close quarters, are a spectacular sight.

The local branches of the Royal Society for the Protection of Birds arrange a full programme of events throughout the year and visitors are always welcome. See **Burhou**.

Brecqhou: Brecqhou lies off the west coast of Sark, separated from its parent island by the Gouliot Passage. It is privately owned on a tenancy from the Seigneur of Sark and the tenant thereby has a seat in the Chief Pleas, the island's legislature.

Budget:

Pot of tea for one in a café	45p
Cup of coffee in a café	65p
Half a pint of beer in pub	50p
Measure of whisky in pub	65p
Glass of wine with a meal	95p
Large loaf of bread	78p
Half a pound of local butter	70p
750 g packet of cornflakes	£1.94
100 g jar of instant coffee	£1.95
40 tea bags	93p

Burhou: Burhou and Little Burhou lie about a mile off Alderney's northwest coast separated by The Swinge, a notoriously dangerous stretch of water. Burhou is now a bird reserve, inhabited mainly by puffins but also with razorbills and the occasional storm petrel. Landing is prohibited during the nesting season (April-mid July), but bird-watchers can arrange to visit the island by contacting the Harbour Office, Alderney, tel: 2620. Facilities on the island are spartan and you must take your own food and water. Boat trips can also be arranged.

Buses: There is a comprehensive network of bus routes on Jersey, running from the Weighbridge Bus Station, St. Helier, tel: 21201, to most parts of the island. Routes are numbered 1-21. Full details and timetables (35p) are available from the bus station.

Guernsey, too, has a regular and frequent service running from St. Peter Port to all corners of the island, with a coastal route during the summer. In winter the bus service finishes at 1800; in summer the latest departure is around 2000, depending on the route. Routes are known by letters A-M and fares are based on distance from St. Peter Port (35-75p). A useful shuttle bus also runs a circular route around town (50p). Timetables and further information can be obtained from Guernseybus, Picquet House, St. Peter Port, tel: 724677.

In the summer months on Alderney there is an infrequent bus service to the island's beaches. Ask at the tourist information office for details (see **Tourist Information**).

Cameras & Photography: The islands are very photo-genic, with plenty of romantic castles and dramatic scenery, but remember to make allowances for bright sunlight and glare when taking pictures. Keep films and cameras out of the heat and away from sand and seawater. All the familiar makes of film are available and you will find them slightly cheaper than on the mainland. The following places will take your films for processing:

Jersey – Fuji One Hour Photo, 3 New St, St. Helier; The Camera Centre, 27 King St, St. Helier.

Guernsey – Grut's, 3 & 5 Le Pollet and 40 High St, St. Peter Port; The Camera Centre, 27 Commercial Arcade, St. Peter Port.

Alderney – Janet Boardman Pharmacy, 38 Victoria St, St. Anne.

Sark – The Gift Shop, The Avenue. Films are sent to Guernsey from here for processing, so it may take a couple of days.

Camping & Caravanning: No caravans or camper vans are allowed on the islands unless the vehicle has been adapted for the use of a disabled person. Whether you bring such a vehicle, or a tent, you must use an authorized camp site. Sites are graded from one to five 'pennants'. The following are some of the authorized sites on the islands:

Jersey – Beuvelande Camp Site, St. Martin, tel: 53575; Quennevais Camp Site, Les Ormes Farm, St. Brelade, tel: 42436; Rozel Camping Park, Summerville Farm, St. Martin, tel: 56797; Summer Lodge, Leoville, St. Ouen, tel: 81921.

Guernsey – Fauxquets Valley Farm Camp Site, Castel, tel: 54460; Vaugrat Camping, route de Vaugrat, St. Sampson's, tel: 57468.

Alderney – Saye Camping Hire Tents, tel: 2914/2556; Alderney Canvas Holidays, tel: 2196.

Sark – La Vallette, tel: 2066; Falles Barn Bar, tel: 2186; Pomme de Chien, tel: 2316.

Herm – Seagull Camping, The Administration Office, tel: 22377.

Car Hire: It is hardly worth taking your own car to the Channel Islands, partly because car hire there is relatively inexpensive and partly because it is very expensive to move a car around the islands or to France by ferry. All the national hire firms , such as Avis, Hertz, Budget, etc. are represented, and some of the local firms are listed below. Typical rates might be £14-20 per day in the height of the season.
Jersey – You will need to be over 22 and have held a valid driving licence without endorsements for dangerous or drunken driving for the last five years. Holiday Hire Cars, 4-5 Parade, St. Helier, tel: 20464/5; Joyride Self-Drive Hire, Gorey Hill, Gorey, tel: 53863; Leisure Drive Ltd, Perth House, St. Aubin, tel: 43236/7; Zebra Hire Cars, Esplanade, St. Helier, tel: 36556; Premier Hire Cars, D'Auberts Garage, St. Brelade's Bay, tel: 42283.
Guernsey – Age and insurance requirements vary from company to company. A1 Car Hire, North Esplanade, St. Peter Port, tel: 712228; Baubigny Hire Cars, Baubigny, St. Sampson's, tel: 45855; Economy

Cars, rue du Pré, St. Peter Port, tel: 726926; Falles Hire Cars, Airport Rd, Forest, tel: 36902.
Alderney – Alderney Hire Cars, 8 Braye St, St. Anne, tel: 2611/2992; Star Rent-a-Car, tel: 2727; Grand Self-Drive, tel: 2848.

Casquets, The: This vicious group of rocks lies a few miles to the west of Alderney, right on the northwest corner of continental Europe. The Casquets have claimed many notable wrecks, including the *White Ship* in 1120, the *Victory* in 1744 and the *Stella* in 1899. The 120-ft lighthouse sends out one of the most powerful beams in the world.

Castles & Fortifications: Being strategically placed at the mouth of the English Channel between France and Britain, it is not surprising that the islands have been fortified by every successive wave of inhabitants, from prehistory to the present. There are earthworks dating from the early Iron Age throughout the islands (see **GUERNSEY-PREHISTORIC SITES, JERSEY-MUSEUMS, JERSEY-PREHISTORIC SITES**), a Roman fort on Alderney known as the Nunnery (see **ALDERNEY-WHAT TO SEE**), and the Vikings also left their mark with a headland fort at Jerbourg. The loss by King John of mainland Normandy resulted in the building of the great castles of Mont Orgueil (see **JERSEY-BUILDINGS**) and Castle Cornet (see **GUERNSEY-BUILDINGS**) which played their part throughout the centuries

in the ding-dong fighting between France and England. Jersey and Guernsey also have Martello towers dating from the time of Napoleon. Fort Regent (see **JERSEY-CHILDREN**) dates from the early 1800s. Alderney saw perhaps the most concerted effort to fortify the islands against the French in the 1850s when the huge harbour wall at Braye and a ring of 18 forts were built around the coast. Midway through this programme the French were defeated by the Prussians and ceased to be a military threat so none of these impressive buildings was ever put to the test. Fort Clonque has been converted to holiday accommodation and is available to let from the Landmark Trust.

Cattle: Channel Island cattle are thought to originate from herds brought from France by monks many centuries ago. Guernsey cattle are slightly bigger than Jerseys and often have white patches. Both are protected by laws which prohibit the importing of any other breed of cattle, keeping the strains pure. Guernseys are also to be found on Alderney, Herm and Sark. They produce extremely rich milk in great quantities and the butter, cream and ice cream made from it is beyond comparison. In the past the cattle were tethered in the fields and milked where they stood but with modern dairy methods this is no longer an economical proposition. Copies of the milk cans used before mechanization took over are sold as souvenirs (see **GUERNSEY-SHOPPING 1**).

Chemists: Dispensing chemists on the islands include the following:
Jersey – Roseville Pharmacy, 7 Roseville St, St. Helier (0900-2130
Mon.-Sat.; 0930-1300, 1400-2130 Sun. & bank hol.).
Guernsey – Boots the Chemist, 47-49 High St, St. Peter Port;
Lloyd's Ltd, 22 States Arcade, St. Peter Port; Stonelakes, 2 The Bridge,
St. Sampson's; J. L. Bourget, The Pharmacy, Route de Carteret, Côbo.
A list of chemists which are open on Sun. appears in the local press.
Alderney – J. Boardman, The Pharmacy, 38 Victoria St, St. Anne,
tel: 2126. See **Health**.

Children: The islands are a paradise for children. There are sandy
beaches, medieval castles and quiet lanes for cycling and horse riding.
There are major indoor leisure complexes on both Jersey and Guernsey
offering all kinds of exciting distractions.
Children are made very welcome at hotels and restaurants on all the
islands and many offer reduced rates for shared rooms, and small
portions at mealtimes. Most attractions have something to amuse
children and some have crèche facilities. Many car-hire firms offer free
children's seats and it is also possible to hire pushchairs, prams, cots
and high chairs. On Jersey, try Doubledays Pushchair Hire, 19 Stopford
Rd, St. Helier, tel: 31505, or The Hire Shop at Millbrook, tel: 73699, or
Hastings Rd, tel: 77775.
Guernsey has a Holiday Play Scheme Association, tel: 27211. Cots and
pushchairs can be hired from Born Again, Piette Stores, Piette Rd, St.
Peter Port, tel: 23002; Perrio's, Wardleys, Beaucoup Lane, tel: 54178;
The Hire Shop, Charroterie Mills, tel: 28218. See **GUERNSEY-CHILDREN**,
JERSEY-CHILDREN, **Baby-sitters**.

Churches: Jersey has been divided into 12 parishes and Guernsey
into ten for over 1000 years, and there is evidence that the earliest
chapels were built around AD 500. All the present church buildings
have been added to throughout their history, many incorporating parts
of the pagan shrines which may have formed their foundations. Every
church on the islands has an interesting history so it is worth calling in
if you have a few moments to spare. See **GUERNSEY-CHURCHES**, **JERSEY-
CHURCHES**.

Vazon Bay, Guernsey

Climate: Being so far south and well clear of the mainland it is no wonder that the Channel Islands claim higher sunshine rates than even the sunniest resorts on the south coast of England. Snow and frost are rare, though it can be slow to warm up in spring, and sea fogs are not uncommon in May and June. Rainfall, at around 35 inches per annum, is higher than London but lower than the West Country, and the Aug. mean temperature is about 17°C. The islands can also be windy, so for the best information listen to the shipping forecast on Radio 4, then head for the sheltered beaches.

Credit Cards: See **Money**.

Crime & Theft: Take the same precautions against theft as you would anywhere else on holiday: leave valuables in the hotel safe, lock your possessions out of sight in your car, and don't leave anything unattended on the beach. Many reports of lawbreaking, particularly drunk driving, unruly behaviour and minor theft, are connected with alcohol and spoilt, bored youths. In order to combat this problem, licensing laws have had to be tightened up and alcohol is not quite as cheap as it was. See **Emergency Numbers**, **Insurance**, **Police**.

Currency: Jersey and Guernsey both issue their own notes and coins which circulate alongside and on a par with the pound sterling. Pound notes are still in use. Channel Islands coins are not legal tender in Britain so it is a good idea to change your money before you return home. See **Money**.

Customs Allowances: See **Passports & Customs**.

Dentists: See **Health**.

Disabled People: The Jersey Tourism Department publishes a list which details the availability of lifts, ground-floor apartments and other facilities in island accommodation. The Guernsey Tourist Board, too, distributes a very useful booklet called *Access in Guernsey – a Guide for Physically Disabled Residents and Visitors*, which is packed with useful information, including hotels and restaurants which particularly welcome disabled visitors, not only on Guernsey but also on Alderney and Sark. Guernsey Association of the Disabled, tel: 724102/722435 can also offer advice. There are special parking zones in St. Helier for the disabled, but you must obtain a disabled-parking certificate from the appropriate office in the town hall. See **Health**, **Insurance**.

Drinks: Most of the familiar soft drinks, wines and spirits are available throughout the islands, and there are also some local brews to try. On Jersey, Randalls produce a full range of beers; from low-alcohol through IPA (India Pale Ale) and Randalls Gold (a lightly hopped, refreshing real ale) to Best, Original VB (Very Best, which is strong and dark) and Stout. Visits can be made by arrangement to their brewery in Clare St, St. Helier, tel: 73541. Ann Street Brewery produces the famous Mary Ann beer which appears on many pub signs. Visits to their brewery at 57 Ann St, St. Helier, tel: 31561, are also by arrangement only. La Mare Vineyards, St. Mary, tel: 81178, were established in the early 1970s and sell their own wines and ciders by the glass and by the bottle (1000-1730 Mon.-Fri., May-mid Oct).
There are two breweries on Guernsey. Randalls have been brewing here also since 1868 and can be found at the Vauxlaurens Brewery, St.

Julian's Ave, St. Peter Port, tel: 20134. Tours are by appointment only. The Guernsey Brewery dates back to 1845 and today has some eight beers on its lists, including Pony Ales, with its Real Draught Bitter topping the tables for the strongest real ale in the Channel Islands. Guided tours of the premises, on South Esplanade, St. Peter Port, take place morning and afternoon on weekdays in the summer months; tel: 20143. There is no grape wine produced on the island but Guernsey Tomato Museum sells a tomato wine (see **GUERNSEY-MUSEUMS**).

Driving: There are miles of roads and country lanes crisscrossing the islands. The main roads on Jersey circle the island but most of the roads are narrow, leafy lanes meandering through fields, woods and villages. These lanes are a delight to explore and will lead you to plenty of unexpected discoveries. Guernsey is more open but the lanes are just as narrow and sinuous, so do take care. Alderney is so small it is hardly worth driving, while Sark has sensibly banned all cars! Visitors must have a valid certificate of insurance and an up-to-date driving licence. Traffic drives on the left here and most UK traffic laws apply, though there are some differences: you must give way at a yellow 'stop' line, and there are 'filter-in-turn' junctions, where you take your turn with other vehicles in joining or crossing a stream of traffic. On Jersey the maximum speed is 40 mph, with areas of 20 and 30 mph, which are signposted. On Guernsey and Alderney the maximum speed limit is 35 mph but in town it is 25 mph and can fall as low as 5 mph in places. The Island Traffic Committee, PO Box 106, Rosaire Ave, St. Peter Port, tel: 712881, issues a leaflet about driving on the islands (also available from police stations, tourist information offices and car-hire companies). See **Accidents & Breakdowns**, **Car Hire**, **Parking**, **Petrol**.

Drugs: All drugs are illegal and there are severe penalties for offenders.

Eating Out: Eating out on the Channel Islands is one of the great pleasures of a visit here. Not only is the bill smaller because of the lack of VAT (Value-Added Tax) and the reduced duty on wine, but the quality of the fresh produce which goes into the meal is without equal. Price categories used in the **RESTAURANTS** pages are based on a three-

course meal with wine for one person and are as follows:
Expensive: over £15; Moderate: £10-15; Inexpensive: under £10. See
GUERNSEY-RESTAURANTS, **JERSEY-RESTAURANTS**, **Food**.

Ecrehous, The: This reef of rocky islands lies about five miles off
Jersey's northeast coast, about halfway between the island and mainland France, which claimed possession as recently as the 1950s. There
are three main islands, Maître Île where there are the ruins of a chapel,
Marmotière, which boasts an old Customs House, and Blanc Île, where
there are a few holiday cottages. There are signs of periodic habitation
dating from prehistoric times, but today you will find people there only
in fine, settled weather.

Electricity: 240 volts AC, as in the UK, using square-pin plugs.

Emergency Numbers: Dial 999 at any time in an emergency. The following are local numbers for the emergency services and other organizations.
Jersey – Police, tel: 75511; Ambulance, tel: 72222; Fire, tel: 37444.
Guernsey – Police, tel: 725111; Ambulance, tel: 725211; Fire, tel: 724491; Samaritans, tel: 715515.
Alderney – Police, tel: 2731; Hospital, tel: 2822; Harbour Office, tel: 2620.
Sark – Medical Centre, tel: 2045; Harbour Master, Maseline Harbour, tel: 2323.

Events:
March: Jersey Jazz Festival.
April: Jersey Pro-Am Golf Tournament.
April/May: Jersey Spring Festival, with special markets, shopping promotions, shows, exhibitions, dancing, concerts and bands, and special events throughout the island.
May: Jersey International Air Rally, with some 80 planes from all over Europe gathering at the airport; Guernsey Jazz Festival; Jersey Good

Food Festival with tastings, demonstrations and gala events culminating in the Salon Culinaire when the island's chefs are judged by an international panel.

June: Guernsey International Dance Festival.

August: Jersey's Battle of Flowers (see **A–Z**); Guernsey's North Show, a similar extravaganza to the Battle of Flowers; Guernsey Marathon.

September: European Water-Ski Racing Championships at Jersey's St. Aubin's Bay; Jersey International Festival of Traditional Music, Song and Dance, a three-day programme of concerts and ceilidhs in People's Park.

September/October: Festival France-Jersey, comprising traditional events, including street theatre and concerts.

October: Alderney Fishing Festival.

November: Jersey Marathon.

Excursions: The coast of mainland France can seem so near on a clear day that it is a great temptation to nip over for a short stay during your holiday. Don't forget your passport and if you take advantage of Condor's offer of a hired car to meet you at the French end you will need your driving licence. If you ship your car on the Morvan Fils Commodore Car Ferry Service you will, of course, need continental documentation for the vehicle.

Air France and Jersey European fly to Paris, and Aurigny fly to Cherbourg. Several companies operate a variety of sea crossings to various French ports; consult a local travel agent for details.

Apart from these scheduled flights and ferries, there is a large number of inclusive tours available from Jersey. For example, 'A Taste of Brittany', with Condor, includes the ferry crossings, a guided coach tour to a market, to Dinard, St. Malo and the obligatory stop at a hypermarket. Others will take you to the extraordinary Mont St. Michel or to medieval Dinan, to Cancale or Chateau de Combourg. Prices are very reasonable, from around £20-30 per person depending on the length of the tour. Again, local travel agents have full details.

From Guernsey you can fly to Cherbourg or Dinard with Aurigny, tel: 23474/37426 for further details. Condor, tel: 726121, runs a hydrofoil service from St. Peter Port to St. Malo.

From Alderney there are flights to Dinard and Cherbourg via Guernsey by Aurigny, tel: 2886/2609/2888. In the summer a ferry sails to the little port of Goury on the Cherbourg peninsula. Further information can be obtained from Raymond Travel, Alderney, tel: 2881/2879.
Condor's hydrofoil operates from Sark to St. Malo via Jersey.

Fishing: All the islands offer the sea angler plenty of excitement, and Jersey and Guernsey also have freshwater fishing. There are sandy bays and rocky coasts with overfalls, reefs and tidal races which also offer wreck fishing. In summer expect mackerel, garfish, wrasse, pollack, plaice, sole, turbot and bass, while in winter vast shoals of mullet feed around the islands and conger and tope of record sizes come close to the shore. For freshwater fishing for rudd, roach, perch, carp, bream, tench and chub try Millbrook Reservoir and South Canal, St. Ouen; for trout (by fly only), go to Vale de La Mare Reservoir, St. Ouen, Jersey. Permits are available from PJN Fishing Tackle, 7 Beresford Market, St. Helier.

Food: The Channel Islands have long been famous for their dairy produce, their fresh vegetables – particularly tomatoes – and for wonderfully fresh fish in great variety. There is a local shellfish known as the ormer (from the French *oreille de mer*, meaning 'ear of the sea') which is very rare and can only be collected at very low spring tides, though it is now successfully being farmed on Guernsey at Rocquaine Bay (see **GUERNSEY-SHOPPING 2**). The single shell is held to the underside of rocks by a large muscle which is the edible part – after it has been well pounded and cooked by someone who knows how to prepare it!

Look out, too, for the *gâche*, a type of doughy fruit cake which is a local speciality found in cake shops throughout Guernsey.

Jersey has gained a reputation for its high standards in restaurants encouraged by the wealthy inhabitants and visitors from neighbouring France. This is reflected in the annual Good Food Festival (see **Events**) when chefs compete openly for much-coveted awards. See **GUERNSEY-RESTAURANTS, JERSEY-RESTAURANTS, Eating Out**.

German Occupation: It was decided by the British government some time after World War I that it would be impractical to defend the Channel Islands if war broke out again, particularly as air power had become a force to be reckoned with. Consequently, in 1940, with the Germans already in France, the islands were demilitarized and those who wished to leave were evacuated. The Germans were informed that the islands were undefended on 28 June 1940 and by 4 July all were occupied by Nazi troops. The Channel Islands were to be a major part of the Germans' western bastion known as the Atlantic Wall; monumental earthworks, concrete bunkers, tank-proof seawalls and gun emplacements are the legacy of this set of defences which seemed almost indestructible. The human toll was high: prisoners of war were used as forced labourers and there was a concentration camp on

German Underground Hospital

Alderney. The islanders also began to feel the effects of their isolation once the Allies started to regain their grip on Europe. In Sep. 1944 the Germans announced that food and medical supplies for the civilian population were exhausted but it was not until after Christmas that the SS *Vega* was allowed into St. Peter Port, relieving a much worried and undernourished population. On the morning of 9 May 1945, two days after the surrender of the German High Command, surrenders were signed in Guernsey and Jersey, followed by the arrival of British troops. The next day the Union Jack was raised in Royal Sq., St. Helier. Today you can visit many of the German fortifications which have been retained as museums, legacies of the Occupation and chilling reminders of the Nazis' presence on the islands. See **GUERNSEY-MUSE-UMS**, **JERSEY-BUILDINGS**, **JERSEY-MUSEUMS**.

Golf: Good weather and the pleasant countryside make golf popular with both residents and visitors but you must book ahead if you want to play.
Jersey – La Moye Golf Club, St. Brelade, tel: 43401: 6267 yd, SSS 70. First-class links course which is host to the Jersey Open. You must have a certified handicap card signed by your home club. £22 per round, £30 per day for two rounds, weekends £25 per round. Royal Jersey Golf Club, Grouville, tel: 54416: 6106 yd, SSS 69. You must have a certified handicap card signed by your home club to play here. £22 per round, £30 per day for two rounds; £25 per round at weekends. Les Mielles Golf Course, St. Ouen's Bay: a 12-hole par-3 course, driving range, putting green and crazy golf. £3.50 per two-and-a-quarter-hr round.
Guernsey – Royal Guernsey Golf Club, L'Ancresse Common, Vale, tel: 47022. Bring a certified handicap card signed by your own club. Visitors are not allowed to play on Thu. afternoons or at weekends. £15 per round, all day.
Alderney – Nine-hole course at Les Huguettes, tel: 2853. Green fees here are the lowest on the islands.
Sark and Herm have no golf courses.

Guernsey: When you arrive in Guernsey, whether by sea or by air, you will be aware of the fringe of white water around the coast, beating on the offshore rocks, against the high cliffs of the south and along the Atlantic-facing beaches of the west. The sea has always dictated life here, whether to fishermen and their catches or to smugglers and their contraband. If you miss Guernsey when you're sailing from the east,

the next landfall will be America, so that the full force of the north Atlantic can be felt on Guernsey's west coast, a feature which delights surfers and board sailors and explains why the capital is to be found on the eastern coast.

St. Peter Port has been a haven for seaborne men since early times, but the present harbour did not start to take shape until 1580, when the first sea walls were built. Since then the area protected from wind and wave has been extended century by century until today there is the extensive network of inner and outer harbours, docks and quays that attract the many cargo ships, ferries, fishing boats, yachts and pleasure cruisers that you will see if you take a walk around the port. If you walk out along Castle Pier to take a closer look at Castle Cornet (see **GUERNSEY-BUILDINGS**) you will be able to look across the harbour from the van-tage point of the high wall which backs onto Havelet Bay. The town today has an attractive, seaside-holiday-town atmosphere, but its roots are well bedded in ancient commerce. The recent discovery of Roman warehouses and quays, as well as the wreck of a Roman ship near the harbour entrance, have given credence to the idea that St. Peter Port was an important trading post and victualling station for merchantmen from the Mediterranean. It was during the late 18th and early 19thC that the Town, as it is known to everyone on the island, really blos-somed and saw a great deal of classic and stylish building which still

survives. The main shopping area, around Le Pollet, Smith St and High St, is still cobbled for much of its length and all the stores are small and almost imitimate when compared to mainland malls.

There is an atmosphere of quiet gentility about Guernsey which probably attracts slightly more circumspect visitors than neighbouring Jersey, such as families who are not expecting too much entertainment, but who want more of an old-fashioned seaside holiday with a bit of island romance thrown in. The countryside is not particularly exciting but nevertheless offers miles of quiet lanes where you can walk or cycle without too much danger of being run down, though there are far too many cars on the island for its own good. The coastal walks and acres of sandy beaches on the west coast are without parallel in the Channel Islands and the whole island is now geared to providing food and distractions for wet days.

Guernsey is also a good stepping-off point for visiting other islands and France is within easy reach (see **Excursions**). Alderney and Jersey are within 15 minutes' flying time. Herm, Sark and Jersey can all be reached by ferry from St. Peter Port. But it is worth giving Guernsey plenty of time as it has a great deal to offer within its few square miles, in terms of varied scenery, historical landmarks, wild bird and plant life, watersports, good eating and the same exceptionally fine weather that is the hallmark of these islands.

Health: It is foolhardy to travel without valid insurance providing substantial accident and health cover, as the cost of falling ill on holiday can be so expensive. Any visitor to Jersey can consult a local GP or dentist, but is expected to pay the cost of the consultation and medicines prescribed. No reimbursement is made by the DSS for this. Residents of the UK requiring treatment during a visit to the Bailiwick of Guernsey are entitled to free medical, dental and nursing services, physiotherapy (if prescribed by a local practitioner) and the use of the pharmaceutical service, presently 80p per prescribed item. Visitors cannot be helped with the costs of repatriation to the mainland. On Sark you will be charged for consultations and prescriptions so you should have insurance cover. In emergencies a fast St. John Ambulance launch will take patients to Guernsey where that island's regulations apply. Hospitals on the islands are as follows:

Jersey – The General Hospital, Gloucester St, St. Helier, tel: 71000, has an Accident & Emergency department. For less serious problems there is a free clinic for advice and treatment (0900-1200 Mon.-Sat., May-Sep.; 0900-1130 Mon., Wed., Fri., Oct.-April). Prescriptions are £1 per item.

Guernsey – The Princess Elizabeth Hospital, tel: 725241; Castel Hospital, tel: 725241; King Edward VII Hospital, tel: 725241.

Alderney – Mignot Memorial Hospital, tel: 2822.

Doctors on the islands are as follows:

Jersey – For a full list of practices, consult the local telephone directory.

Guernsey – Albany Medical Partnership, Albany House, Ruette Braye, St. Peter Port, tel: 25121; Côbo Surgery, Route de Carteret, tel: 56404; St. Martin's Surgery, Les Merriennes, tel: 37757; Grange End Surgery, The Grange, St. Peter Port, tel: 24184; Le Longfrie Surgery, rue de Longfrie, St. Peter's, tel: 64185; L'Aumone Surgery, Castel, tel: 56517; Grandes Maisons Road Surgery, St. Sampson's, tel: 45915; Rohais Surgery, Rohais, St. Peter Port, tel: 23322; Ann's Place Surgery, Ann's Place, St. Peter Port, tel: 711237.

Alderney – There are two medical practices, tel: 2494 and 2077.

Sark – Sark Medical Centre, tel: 2045.

See **Disabled People**, **Emergency Numbers**, **Insurance**.

Herm: You can see Herm clearly to the northwest of St. Peter Port, the hump of the southern part of the island standing out clear against the sky. It is a 20-min boat trip across the Little Russel Channel, twisting between reefs and rocks and passing the strange tower of Brehon which completely covers the island on which it was built back in 1856 as a defence against the French. The boat will probably take you into the little harbour on the west coast of Herm, unless the tide is a long way out, in which case it will go to the Rosière steps to the south.

The present tenant of Herm, Major Peter Wood, is exploiting the island's commercial potential, and much of his success to date is attributable to the large herd of Guernsey cattle which are kept here. The first ferry of the day is known as the milk boat: get up early to catch it and you can have up to 11 hr on Herm at a special low price.

As you leave the boat you will find the White House Hotel and Restaurant, a few shops and the Mermaid Tavern, almost the sum total of the gesture to tourism and quite adequate! People come here in

droves at the height of summer in good weather but it is surprising how quickly they fan out and disappear. You can hire a bicycle or just walk (there are no motor vehicles) but with few roads and a perimeter length of around three miles part of the joy of this visit is strolling in the utter peace and quiet. By the sea you may well see puffins, while on the gorse there will be stonechats. In the spring look out for the tiny Burnett rose and the white star-of-Bethlehem.

There is a footpath right around the coast which you can walk easily in a morning, with plenty of tracks along which to take a short cut if you get tired. The southern part of the island is rugged, but the highest point is only 65 ft above sea level. From Point Sauzebourge you can see Jethou (see **A-Z**), while to the east are the bastion-like cliffs of Sark. The north is low and sandy, capped by the Common which is inhabited by rabbits and banked with dunes. The centre of the island is the most temperate and where you will find the best of the pastureland, the settlements and most of the trees. The whole island is very well sign-posted so it is quite impossible to get lost! See **HERM-WHAT TO SEE**.

How to get there: by sea – from Guernsey Herm Seaway, opposite the Town Church, St. Peter Port, tel: 24161. Boats run daily in summer, with special afternoon and evening cruises (£5, child £2.50) from Guernsey Trident, Weighbridge Clocktower, tel: 721379. There are also special excursions for evening meals at The Ship, for pub or restaurant lunches, and for evening barbecues at The Mermaid.

History: Throughout their history the islands have been closely linked with France, as you will notice from many of the place names and from the surnames of the locals. In AD 933 the islands became the property of William, Duke of Normandy, and after the Norman Conquest in 1066 they became subject to rule from England. In spite of the loss of mainland Normandy by King John early in the 13thC, the islands remained loyal to the English crown and for centuries combatted French attacks, none of which resulted in permanent occupation. In the mid-15thC the islands acquired the right of neutrality which they were to retain until 1689. William of Orange, however, abolished this neutrality, opening another period of skirmishes with the French. During the revolution in France many refugees escaped to the islands and some remained. In the 18th and early 19thCs the islands' economy thrived on smuggling and privateering, with English attempts to introduce the custom-house system failing dismally. During Victorian times the islands flourished, making money from stone quarrying, oyster farming and cider making. The Queen herself also visited on several occasions, leaving a host of renamed landmarks in her wake, such as Victoria Tower on Guernsey and Royal Bay of Grouville (see **JERSEY-BEACHES**). The German Occupation (see **A-Z**) put the islands under a foreign power for the first time in centuries and resulted in much hardship for the islanders. Today, however, the economy thrives on the profits of tourism, financial wizardry and quality agricultural produce, exploiting to the full the advantages of 'offshore' status, a benign climate and the islands' position as stepping stones to Europe. See **Prehistory**.

Horse Riding: A delightful way to see the islands is from the back of a horse, high above the walls and hedges of the narrow lanes. For tuition and escorted hacks, try the following:
Jersey – Bon-Air Stables, St. Lawrence, tel: 65196; Brabant Riding School, Brabant, Trinity, tel: 61105; Le Clair Stables, Sunnydale, rue Militaire, St. John, tel: 62823; Sorrel Centre, Mont Fallu, St. Peter, tel: 42009.
Guernsey – La Carrière Stables, tel: 49998; Guernsey Equestrian Centre, tel: 725257; Otterbourne Riding Centre, tel: 63085; Les Adams Farm, tel: 65358.
Sark – Supervised hacking with Joanne Crossley; ask at your hotel.

Îles Chausey: A group of rocks and islets which are considered to be part of Jersey even though they are only nine miles from the French coast at Granville. Grande Île has until very recently been permanently inhabited by fishermen-farmers.

Insurance: You should take out travel insurance covering you against theft and loss of property and money, as well as medical expenses, for the duration of your stay. Your travel agent should be able to recommend a suitable policy. See **Crime & Theft**, **Driving**, **Health**.

Jersey: Jersey is the largest and furthest south of the whole group of the Channel Islands. Its east coast is only some 15 miles from from France which is easily visible on all but the mistiest of days. Throughout its history the island has been subject to squabbles with the French and the huge castles and fortifications all around the coast tell their own story. The German Occupation (see **A-Z**) also left a vast legacy of concrete which will never be eroded, particularly since so much of it has now been caught up in the tourist trade, with bunkers converted to museums and underground chambers opened to the public.

But the sunshine and year-round warmth have given Jersey the means to rise above such grey periods in the island's past. Early flowers and the best new potatoes in the world remind many mainlanders of this little patch of spring when they are still fighting off the last clutches of winter. Today, however, the island is famous as much for its financial status as for its produce, and can probably name more millionaires per square mile than most places.

This affluence is not all necessarily native – a great many people have chosen to move to Jersey to make the most of the island's low income-tax levels. There are facilities to cater for the richest tastes here but don't be misled into thinking that entertainment, restaurants and hotels only cater for the very wealthy – there is plenty going on for everyone and the island tourist office is doing a very good job of advertising the attractions of Jersey for family vacations, short breaks and activity and adventure holidays, as well as for the luxury end of the market.

On arrival, Jersey can look very built up and it does have an extremely high-density population, but it is surprising how quickly you can leave the urban areas of St. Helier and the south and get out into relatively open countryside with agricultural land and scattered farmhouses, open marshland, sand dunes and beaches to the west and more rugged and steep cliffs and valleys on the north coast with ancient fishing coves squatting between headlands. Jersey experienced tremendous growth and popularity during late Georgian and early Victorian times which lent an elegant air to much of the building, particularly in St. Helier and around Gorey, although the more modern sprawls, which are the blight of every populous country, are less attractive.

Jersey has much to offer the out-of-season visitor as well as the sun-seeker, but this is not really the place to come for a truly get-away-from-it-all holiday. There are a huge number of cars around, both local and hired, so walking along main roads can be a bit fraught. In more rural areas there are no pavements, so until you get onto footpaths and country lanes, do take care. The tourist office produces several booklets which give excellent maps and directions for quiet country and seaside walks as well as guides for naturalists and birdwatchers. Sports enthusiasts also are well catered for with water sports, and especially yachting, particularly popular.

The island has excellent sea and air links with the mainland and the other islands. And of all the islands, this is the place which will appeal if you like a lively holiday, with a vast choice of restaurants, an active nightlife, excellent shopping and entertainment facilities.

Jethou: Jethou is privately owned and is not open to the public. You can get a good view of it from Point Sauzebourge at the southern end of Herm. The manor house is on the northwest coast and the writer Sir Compton Mackenzie was the tenant here from 1920 to 1934.

Langtry, Lillie (1852-1929): Jersey's most famous daughter, Emilie Charlotte Le Breton, was born at the rectory in St. Saviour where her father was the incumbent. Lillie was her nickname and she acquired the surname Langtry on her marriage to her first husband, Edward, who died in 1897. She was both beautiful and sociable and her friendship with the Prince of Wales attracted a great deal of public attention. Her work as an actress took her all over Europe, to America and South Africa. She died in Monte Carlo and is buried in St. Saviour's churchyard (see **JERSEY-CHURCHES**). See **JERSEY-MUSEUMS**.

Language: The Norman-French dialects spoken here for centuries are dying out now and everyone speaks English, but it is not long since French was the official language. Many islanders speak good French and there are strong societies on the islands aimed at preserving ties with France and encouraging local dialects.

Laundries: In addition to the laundrettes below, most hotels also offer laundry facilities.

Jersey – First Tower Launderette, St. Aubin's Rd, St. Helier; Wash 'n' Shop, 5 Five Oaks Parade, St. Saviour; Give-it-a-Whirl, Grève d'Azette, St. Clement; Besco Laundry, Beaumont, St. Peter.

Guernsey – Burtols, South Esplanade, St. Peter Port (10 lb of laundry for £5.50, ironing 30p per item); coin-operated laundrette behind Wyndham's Hotel, Glategny Esplanade, St. Peter Port (0730-2230).

Alderney – Alderney Laundry and Dry Cleaning, tel: 3188.

Lihou: Lihou is connected to Guernsey at low tide by a causeway nearly half a mile long which runs out from the headland at L'Erée, but you must not attempt this walk on a rising tide (see **Tides & Currents**). There are the remains of the Priory of St. Mary of the Rocks on the south coast but today the island is run as a commercial farm.

Lost Property: If you have lost something, report it at the reception desk of your hotel. If the loss is serious, report it to the local police and remember to get a copy of your statement for insurance purposes. See **Insurance**.

Markets: There is a street market on Thu. afternoons in St. Peter Port on Guernsey, when the stall-holders wear traditional Victorian costume and sell everything from bric-a-brac to Guernsey seconds. Both St. Helier (see **JERSEY-SHOPPING 1**) and St. Peter Port also have splendid Victorian markets which you will find are the best places in which to buy fresh food and produce.

Minquiers, Les: Known locally as the Minkies, this reef of rocks lies 12 miles south of Jersey, about halfway to Dinard and St. Malo, and is another territory which was disputed with the French until recently. The French still hold their traditional fishing rights around the islands and Maitresse Île, the largest, provides shelter and a landing place for fishermen. In the past granite quarrying and seaweed collecting (see **Vraic**) have attracted people but today the islands are largely uninhabited.

Money: Banking hours on Jersey are normally 0930-1530 Mon.-Fri. but, as you would expect in such a major financial centre, there are variations. The major world banks are represented in St. Helier, and there are branches of all the familiar high-street banks throughout the island.
All the British high-street banks also have branches in St. Peter Port on Guernsey and many have branches in St. Martin's and St. Sampson's. Hours are 0930-1530 Mon-Fri.
Banking hours on Alderney are 0930-1300, 1430-1530 Mon-Fri. Lloyds, Midland and National Westminster all have branches in St. Anne. The Trustee Savings Bank (TSB) is open 0930-1230, 1330-1600 Mon.-Thu. and 0930-1230, 1330-1800 Fri.
On Sark, Midland and National Westminster have branches at La Collinette with opening hours of 1000-1230, 1400-1500 Mon.-Fri. Thomas Cook Ltd has a branch at Le Pollet, St. Peter Port, Guernsey, tel: 725080. Major credit cards are accepted throughout the islands. See **Currency**.

Music: Folk and jazz are well represented on the islands. Tourist information offices (see **A-Z**) will provide details of local clubs and events. Traditional Jersey Lillies and Helier Morris Men put on dancing displays throughout the island in the summer, for example at Gorey Pier, St. Helier Town Precinct and Portelet.
A major hub of Guernsey's social and cultural life is St. James Concert Hall in St. Peter Port, where a wide variety of musical, dramatic and social events are staged, featuring local and visiting artistes. Details in local press (see **Newspapers**). See GUERNSEY-NIGHTLIFE, GUERNSEY-PUBS, JERSEY-NIGHTLIFE.

Natural History: The flora and fauna of the Channel Islands are subtly different from mainland Britain, being significantly further south, warmer, and nearer to continental Europe. Also, the individual islands parted company from Europe at different times, allowing each to keep its own particular characteristics. Alderney is flat and sandy and does not offer much shelter, Sark is steep with precipitous cliffs, Jersey slopes to the south, and Guernsey slopes to the north. Jersey, which separated from France after the other islands, has moles, grass snakes, green lizards, newts and toads, while moles, foxes, squirrels and hares never reached Guernsey. Island floral specialities include the Jersey Orchid, buttercup, cudweed, thrift and the belladonna lily, also known as the Jersey Lily. On Guernsey look for the Guernsey Centaury and the Guernsey Fern, the giant echium and the Guernsey Lily, rich red and said to have come originally from Japan. See **Bird-watching**.

Newspapers: The *Jersey Evening Post* is published six days a week and has a sister paper, the *Jersey Weekly Post*. The *Guernsey Evening Press & Star* is also published six days a week, while the *Guernsey Weekly Press* comes out on Fri. and *Weekender* is published on Sat. Alderney's *The Journal* appears every fortnight. UK and major European dailies are available with the first flights of the day. See **What's On**.

Opening Times:
Banking hours: See **Money**.
Licensing hours:
Jersey – 0900-2200 Mon.-Sat., 1200-1400, 2000-2400 Sun.
Guernsey – 1030-2200 Mon.-Sat., restricted restaurant licence only Sun.
Alderney – 1000-2400 Mon.-Sat., 1200-1400, 2000-2400 Sun.
Sark – 1000-2200 Mon.-Sat., winter; 1000-2300 Mon.-Sat., summer;
restricted restaurant licence only Sun.
Shops: 0900-1730 as a rule, but hours may be extended to 2000 or
2100 in summer, and there may be lunch hours and half-day closing
(Thu.) in winter.

Orientation: Geologically the Channel Islands are closely related to
neighbouring Normandy and are made up of similar ancient rocks. It
was only around 12,000 years ago, at the end of the last ice age, that
the area was flooded by melting glaciers and the high ground became
the islands.
The most northerly group, comprising Alderney (see **A-Z**), Burhou (see
A-Z), Ortac (see **Bird-watching**), The Casquets (see **A-Z**) and numerous
other rocks and islets, lies less than ten miles west of Cap de la Hague,
separated from France by the Alderney Race, one of the world's most
ferocious tidal races, frequently running at upwards of six knots (see
Tides & Currents). The highest point on Alderney is only 294 ft above
sea level and there are few valleys to offer shelter from the almost
constant wind.
The second, and most westerly group is made up of Guernsey (see **A-Z**)
and a few islets off its west coast including Lihou (see **A-Z**) and, to the
east, Herm (see **A-Z**) and Jethou (see **A-Z**), Sark (see **A-Z**) and Brecqhou
(see **A-Z**). Guernsey is the second-largest of the Channel Islands with a
land area of 24.5 square miles and it has long been associated with
tomato growing and dairy farming. The island slopes towards the north,
with high cliffs along its southern coast and miles of sandy beaches to
the north and west. Across another dangerous stretch of water, known
as the Little Russel Channel, are the tiny islands of Jethou and Herm,
the latter famous for its remarkable shell beach. The Great Russel
Channel separates Herm from Sark, noted for its cliffs and caves, and its

almost feudal outlook. To the southeast of the group is the largest and most sophisticated of the islands, Jersey (see **A-Z**). Fertile and prosperous, Jersey slopes gently towards the south, attracting an average of eight hr of sunshine a day in the summer, allowing grapes, figs and peaches to ripen outdoors. The northern coast is indented and rocky, with numerous sandy bays and high, dramatic cliffs, while the south and west boast immense stretches of sand at St. Ouen and St. Aubin. Off the northeast coast are The Ecrehous (see **A-Z**) and to the south Les Minquiers (see **A-Z**), outposts that complete the Channel Islands archipelago which spans some 60 miles from north to south.

Parking: On-street parking on Jersey operates in time zones and you must buy a Pay Card, on sale throughout the island, for use in 20-min and 1-hr zones. There are also plenty of public car parks which are all well signposted. On Guernsey you must obtain a Parking Clock (50p), on sale at police stations, on ferries, at garages or from the tourist information office (see **A-Z**). Set this clock to the time at which you left your car. Parking zones are indicated by circular blue signs and vary from 15 min to 23 hr. There is no charge for parking but a fine of £10 can be levied if you overstay your time limit. Parking is not a problem on Alderney as there are so few cars, though there are some prohibited areas in St. Anne. See **Driving**.

Passports & Customs: Citizens of the UK and Republic of Ireland do not require passports or entry visas, but remember that if you want to take a day trip to France you will need your passport. You cannot buy duty-free goods on your way to the Channel Islands but you can bring back the following duty-free: 200 cigarettes or 50 cigars or 250 grams of tobacco; 1 litre of spirits; 2 litres of wine.

Petrol: Unleaded petrol is widely available, as is diesel fuel. Self-service filling stations are the norm, as on the mainland. See **Driving**.

Police: The States of Jersey Police Force is assisted by parish representatives known as *centeniers*, *vingteniers* and constable's officers who are unpaid, honorary police but nevertheless have considerable powers. Guernsey's police force has its headquarters in St. James' Chambers, St. Peter Port. The police look very much the 'bobby on the beat' with helmets and capes familiar from the mainland in times past. See **Crime & Theft, Emergency Numbers**.

Post Offices:
Jersey – Broad St, St. Helier.
Guernsey – Smith St, St. Peter Port.
Alderney – Victoria St, St. Anne.
Poste Restante facilities are available at the islands' main post offices.

Prehistory: Some of the very best preserved Palaeolithic and Neolithic sites in northwestern Europe are to be found on the Channel Islands. One of the earliest is La Cotte de St. Brelade on Jersey, a cave which was inhabited when the mammoth and woolly rhinoceros were roaming the countryside. When the first farmers arrived in about 5000 BC they lived in village settlements and evolved elaborate rituals in the burying of their dead. The best of the remains, together with explanatory diagrams and models in the museums of each island will give you the clearest background information before you visit the sites. See **GUERNSEY-PREHISTORIC SITES, JERSEY-MUSEUMS, JERSEY-PREHISTORIC SITES**.

Public Holidays: The Channel Islands observe the same public holidays as the UK with the addition of 9 May, Liberation Day, the anniversary of the islands' liberation from the Nazis in 1945.

Rabies: In an attempt to avoid the spread of rabies to the islands, pets which have come from or landed in continental Europe are forbidden. However, pets may be brought in from the UK, Republic of Ireland and Isle of Man without restriction.

Railways: In common with so many places which fell under Victorian influence, railways were built on the Channel Islands, although Alderney has the only one still running today. Built in 1847 and distinguished by a visit from Queen Victoria in 1854, the Alderney Railway (see **ALDERNEY-WHAT TO SEE**) ran from Mannez Quarry to take stone to build the magnificent breakwater at Braye. Today the Alderney Railway Society runs a service from the little station at the back of Braye Bay to the northeastern tip of the island behind Fort Corblets.

Religious Services: Details of religious services are given outside churches as well as in the local press (see **Newspapers**) and at the tourist information office (see **Tourist Information**).

Sark: One of the more inaccessible Channel Islands – you can only get to Sark by going to either Jersey or Guernsey first, and out of season you can only go over on days when a boat runs from Guernsey to take the Sarkese on a shopping trip (normally Wed. or Sat.). The harbours are on the east coast so you are faced by Sark's imposing coastline with impregnable-looking cliffs as you approach from the west. The impression of steepness continues when you disembark and face the uphill climb to the top of the island, but there is always a tractor-powered 'bus' to carry you and your bags for around 40p. However, many people see the lack of traffic as one of the great attractions of Sark, so why not come prepared to walk, let the diesel fumes blow away and the birdsong take their place.

The island has its own unique history and a social system which is quite unlike any other. In 1563 Helier de Carteret came from Jersey with forty families to settle the land and defend it from invaders, and in return he was granted the island by Queen Elizabeth I as a fief. The forty tenements still exist under the direction of the Seigneur.

Not only is the administration straight out of the past but the gravel roadways, the prefab nature of many of the shops and smaller houses, and the absence of cars all give a visitor the feeling that giving in to the 20thC is not in the nature of the islanders. But then you are almost deafened by a generator, nearly run down by a tractor, and offered a hotel with a heated swimming pool and a television in your room, and you realise that the image is really only skin deep.

Sark can be a pretty place to visit on a fine summer's day and you may well have a wonderful walk, a glorious swim, an excellent meal and get a superficial glimpse of the island's life, but you won't get to the heart of the place unless you stay for a while. And it is the visitors who stay longer who find that they are drawn back year after year – somehow the attractions of Sark are subtle and lingering.

How to get there – Condor Hydrofoil, Commodore Shipping Services, 28 Conway St and Albert Quay, St. Helier, tel: 76300 (c. £26); Weymouth Quay, Dorset, tel: 0305-761551 (Mon.-Sat., Mar.-Oct.); Isle of Sark Shipping Company, White Rock, St. Peter Port, tel: 724059 (c. £12); Harbour Office, Sark, tel: 2450 (several boats daily; less frequent in winter).

Shopping: Many people look on shopping as a leisure activity these days and the Channel Islands are probably one of the most pleasant places to come on a shopping spree. Jersey and Guernsey both offer VAT- (Value-Added Tax) and duty-free shopping, giving purchases the appearance of being cheaper than they actually are when you've paid the necessary taxes on your return home. Perhaps the greatest pleasure is the variety of goods on offer, with continental clothes, shoes, food and ambience as well as the familiar high-street stores.

St. Helier is the main shopping centre and its traffic-free, granite-paved streets are a shopper's heaven. There is a pleasing variety of shops, interspersed with cafés and restaurants where you can rest a while. Much of the centre of St. Peter Port is closed to traffic after 1000 and pedestrians enjoy complete freedom in the cobbled streets around the High St and Le Pollet. St. Sampson's is the second-largest shopping centre on Guernsey, followed by St. Martin's.

Alderney, too, has a surprisingly wide array of shops which provide all the services necessary for islanders as well as gift shopping for visitors. Most are to be found in the Victoria St area of St. Anne.

The only shops on Sark are on The Avenue. Bear in mind that everything here has been imported so everyday goods are more expensive than on the main islands. Some taxable goods, such as perfume and spirits, are cheaper, but the selection is limited. See **GUERNSEY-SHOPPING**, **JERSEY-SHOPPING**, **Best Buys**, **Markets**.

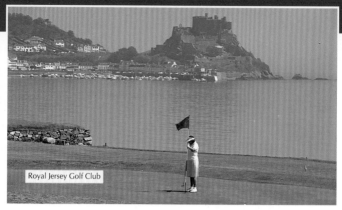

Royal Jersey Golf Club

Sports:

Jersey – Fort Regent, St. Helier, tel: 73000, offers squash, badminton, swimming, indoor bowls, snooker, table tennis, racket ball and pool. There are tennis courts at the Caesarean Tennis Club, Grands Vaux, tel: 79008, and at the Jersey Recreation Grounds, Grève d'Azette, tel: 21938; £3 per hr, racquet and ball hire.

Guernsey – The Beau Sejour Centre offers the widest range of facilities (badminton, squash, roller skating, netball, gymnastics, swimming) and the island boasts the world's fourth-largest indoor-bowls centre at the Guernsey Bowls Stadium. Guernsey Outdoor Pursuits, Dovecot, Les Buissonets, Braye Rd, Vale, tel: 45103, and the Adventure Centre, 29 La Tonnelle, Halfway, St. Sampson, tel: 49601, offer tuition and facilities for archery, orienteering and rock climbing. There is clay-pigeon shooting at La Favorita Hotel, Fermain Bay, St. Martin.

Alderney – There are club facilities for tennis, squash and snooker; windsurfer hire and tuition at Longy Bay and Braye Bay; surfing and wetsuit hire at Corblets Bay. Cricket on the Butes during the summer. Several bowling clubs welcome visiting players: Jersey Bowling Club, Westmount Rd, St. Helier, tel: 32133; St. Brelade Bowling Club, Quennevais, tel: 46894. May–Sep., £2 per session. Crabbe Clay Pigeon Club, St. Mary, tel: 54022, have guns and tuition by a qualified coach. Open Sun. from 1000, Thu. evenings from 1800, Sat. from 1430. 25 clays £2.50. Flying lessons at the Jersey Aero Club, St. Peter, tel: 43990.

Trial introductory lesson £21. Squash courts at Lido de France Squash Club, St. Helier. Non-members must book in person and pay £1.50 deposit. £3.50 for 40 min during the day, £5.50 after 1700. Jersey Squash Club, St. Clement has temporary membership for £3 per week, court fees £1.40 for 40 min. Flying lessons and courses are run by Jersey Aero Club, St. Peter, tel: 43990. There is go-kart racing at Belle Vue Pleasure Park, St. Brelade, tel: 41671. Horse racing takes place at Les Landes, St. Ouen between April and Aug. organized by the Jersey Race Club, tel: 63484. There are the usual course facilities including a licensed bar. See **Fishing**, **Golf**, **Horse Riding**, **Water Sports**.

Taxis: Taxis on the islands are not of a uniform colour or type, but metered cabs have an illuminated sign on the roof.
There are plenty of taxis on Jersey, the main public ranks being at the airport, the Weighbridge, the Parade and at Broad St, St. Helier. However, they are expensive and you can expect to pay £5 for a trip from St. Helier to the airport. Charges increase by 25% after 2300 and by 50% after 0200.
A taxi journey on Guernsey will cost about £1 per mile during the day and slightly more at night. Watch out for add-ons for extra luggage and passengers. There are taxi ranks beside the Town Church and at the Weighbridge, St. Peter Port.
Expect to pay around £5 from the airport to your hotel on Alderney. Local companies include: Alderney Taxis, Braye St and Victoria St, tel: 2611/2992; Mike's Taxis, tel: 3320/3535; St. Anne's Taxi Service, tel: 2000.
On Sark there are no taxis but you can take a horse-drawn cart or the tractor-powered 'bus' from the boat to the top of the hill (40p).

Telephones & Telegrams: Public telephone boxes on the islands are painted yellow (except on Sark, where they are green), and accept 2p, old 5p, 10p, 20p, 50p and £1 coins. They work in the same way as modern mainland payphones. Local calls (standard rate) cost 6p for 5 min, other islands 6p for 50 sec, and the UK 6p for 15 sec. The islands' telephone system is connected to the UK STD system. All the telephone numbers in this guide are given without area codes.

Telegrams can be sent from post-office counters and by telephone; dial 100 and ask the operator for the service.

Television & Radio: All the usual mainland broadcasts can be received in the Channel Islands and in addition there are local stations: BBC Radio Guernsey on 1116kHz or 269 m and 93.2 FM; BBC Radio Jersey on 88.8 FM and 1026kHz; and Channel TV.

Tides & Currents: The English Channel is known for its strong tides and the speed with which the seas get up, but this area and particularly around Alderney is notoriously dangerous. The Cherbourg Peninsula severely narrows the Channel and the water races in and out, causing the whirlpools, overfalls and eddies which are a very real hazard to small boats, swimmers, windsurfers and anyone engaged in water-related activities. The tidal range can be as much as 35 ft and because this rise and fall occurs within a 12-hr cycle you must take great care not to be cut off by the tide. The vast areas of flat sand exposed at low tide can be covered very quickly once the water starts to return. Tide tables are widely available in the shops, and the tourist and harbour masters' offices display times of high tide. If you intend to participate in water sports it is very important to be aware of these problems.

Time Difference: The Channel Islands follow the same time as the UK all year round, i.e. GMT in winter and BST in summer.

Tipping: Many restaurants now add a service charge to their bills, but if they do not, a 10% tip is usual. Taxi drivers and hairdressers expect a tip of about 10%, but remember that the decision is always yours.

Toilets: The islands are well supplied with clean and well kept public toilets. These are marked on leisure maps and details of wheelchair access are given in both Jersey's and Guernsey's guide for physically disabled residents and visitors (see **Disabled People**).

Tourist Information: Tourist information offices on the islands are as follows:
Jersey – Tourism Department, Liberation Sq., St. Helier, tel: 24779 for information; tel: 31958 for accommodation.
Guernsey – Guernsey Tourist Information Bureau, PO Box 23, Whiterock, St. Peter Port, tel: 723555.
Alderney – States Tourist Office, Victoria St/Queen Elizabeth II St, St. Anne. Visitor hot line tel: 2994.
Sark – The Tourism Committee, Information Centre, tel: 2345.
Herm – The Administration Office, tel: 22377.
Jersey Tourism's UK office is at 35 Albemarle St, London W1X 3FB, tel: 071-493 5278.
See **Accommodation**, **Tours**, **What's On**.

Tours: Among several coach companies on Jersey which operate morning (£3), afternoon (£3.50), evening (£3) or all-day tours (£7), with half-price fares for children, are: Blue Coach Tours, 70-72 Colomberie, St. Helier, tel: 22584; Pioneer Coach Tours, Albert St, St. Helier, tel: 25100; and Mascot Motors Ltd, The Weighbridge, St. Helier, tel: 35211. Guernseybus operates a variety of coach tours daily from St. Peter Port: contact Picquet House, St. Peter Port, tel: 724677. Alternatively, try Island Coachways, Les Banques, St. Peter Port, tel: 720210.
Alderney taxi services (see **A–Z**) offer tours by car or minibus, taking in places of interest and beauty.

The best way to see Sark is by horse-drawn carriage with a commentary from the driver (c.£20 for a half-day personal tour), by bicycle (see **Bicycle & Motorcycle Hire**) or on foot. Pat Webb offers a two- to three-hr guided walk – rendezvous in The Avenue. Details can be obtained from your hotel or the tourist information office (see **A-Z**).

Transport: See **Bicycle & Motorcycle Hire, Buses, Car Hire, Excursions, Railways, Taxis, Tours.**

Vraic: *Vraic* is the dialect word for the seaweed which for centuries has been collected around the coasts of the Channel Islands to be used on the fields as fertilizer. In Brittany you can still see farmers with their horses and carts down on the beach collecting seaweed but it is a fairly unusual sight on the islands themselves.

Walking: All the islands are ideal for walkers: there are many lanes and paths unsuitable for traffic, the weather is mild, the bird and plant life plentiful and buses, cafés and refreshments are never too far away. You will need proper walking shoes for the longer cliff walks, a hat in summer and good maps. There are some excellent guides to walking in the islands available from the tourist offices (see **Tourist Information**).

Water Sports:
Parascending – Pilot Watersports, Sugar Basin Slip, St. Aubin's Bay, tel: 63538; Jersey Skywalker Club, tel: 45040. c.£15 per flight.

Sea Angling – Jersey: Fishing trips from St. Helier and Bonne Nuit. Tackle hire from St. Catherine's Breakwater and from Wheways, Broad St, St. Helier. Guernsey: Dougal Lane, Melbourne Cottage, Valnord Hill, St. Peter Port, tel: 727161; Arnold Brehat, l'Abri du Val, Les Villets, Forest, tel: 63730, have boats for hire by the day or longer, for individuals and groups.

Diving – Jersey: Jersey Underwater Centre, Bouley Bay, tel: 61817; Watersports, First Tower, tel: 32813, offers introductory lessons c.£14, six lessons £90, including equipment hire. Guernsey: Sub Aqua Club, Julie Domaille, Le Bordel, La Mazotte, Vale, tel: 49078/45137; Guernsey School of Diving, Tim Morris, Les Quatre Vents, rue des Monts, Delancey, St. Sampson's, tel: 47664/49524.

Sailing – Jersey: Jersey Cruising School, Caledonia House, Caledonia Place, St. Helier, tel: 78522; Longbeach Sailing School, Grouville Bay, tel: 52033. Five-day courses, weekly bareboat and skippered charters; Hobie Cat tuition and hire at Grouville. Guernsey: Royal Channel Islands Yacht Club, St. Peter Port, tel: 25500; David Nicolle, La Colombelle, rue du Hamel, Castel, tel: 64926, offers charters, tuition and day trips.

Surfing – Jersey: Sands Surf & Sail Centre and Watersplash, St. Ouen's Bay, tel: 82885, offers two-hr Malibu board and wetsuit hire £2.50, tuition free. Guernsey: Sarnian Sports, Market Sq., St. Peter Port, tel: 20540, will put you in touch with tutors and give you details of hire facilities.

Water-skiing, surf jets, seasleds, skiboards, hydroslides – Jersey: Jersey Sea Sports Centre, La Haule Slip, St. Aubin, with a skiing trip £8, six lessons £40. Prices include wetsuit and life-jacket hire. Guernsey: Havelet Bay Water-ski School, Les Muguets, Houge Mague Lane, St. Sampson's, tel: 48854.

Windsurfing – Jersey: Jersey Wind & Water Windsurfer Schools, Gunsite, St. Aubin, tel: 42188; Wayside Slip, St. Brelade's Bay, tel: 33388. Beginners' course £35 inclusive of time on a simulator, board hire c.£5 per hr, including wetsuit, and tuition £8. Guernsey: Windsurfing International (West Coast), Côbo, Castel, tel: 53313, and Nautifun, North View L'Ancresse, Vale, tel: 46690, both offer hire and tuition.

What's On: From April to Oct., *What's On Jersey* is available from the tourist information office, and from May to Sep., *Places of Interest* details most of the attractions, while the monthly *Calendar of Events* lists day-by-day events of interest to visitors. In the winter *VIP Magazine* suggests entertainments, sights and restaurants which are open out of season.

Guernsey – An Island for All Seasons is published by the tourist board and includes articles on the main attractions, maps, reviews of exhibitions and new restaurants, as well as plenty of advertisements. *The Islander*, published monthly, has three pages of what's-on listings, together with articles, book reviews and news. Both are free and are widely available in stores and at tourist information offices.

The Alderney Magazine is published regularly at 80p and is full of useful information. See **Events**, **Newspapers**, **Tourist Information**.

Youth Hostels: There are no YHA-associated hostels in the Channel Islands. The cheapest accommodation is bed and breakfast which is available from £9.50 per night, or camping from £2 a night.

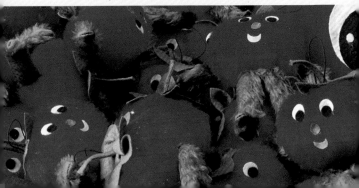